# ALMOST CHOSEN

# ALMOST CHOSEN

## WES DUPIN AND TIM WAY

### FORWORD BY KEVIN HARNEY

*Almost Chosen*
Copyright © 2017 by Wes Dupin

ISBN 978-0-692-88620-5

Scripture quotations marked NLT are taken from the Holy Bible, New Living Translation, copyright © 1996, 2004, 2007, 2013, 2015 by Tyndale House Foundation. Used by permission of Tyndale House Publishers, Inc., Carol Stream, Illinois 60188. All rights reserved New Living Translation.

Scripture quotations marked (NIV) are taken from the Holy Bible, New International Version®, NIV®. Copyright © 1973, 1978, 1984, 2011 by Biblica, Inc.™ Used by permission of Zondervan. All rights reserved worldwide. www.zondervan.com The "NIV" and "New International Version" are trademarks registered in the United States Patent and Trademark Office by Biblica, Inc.™

All rights reserved. No part of this publication may be reproduced, stored in a retrieval system, or transmitted in any form or by any means — electronic, mechanical, photocopy, recording, scanning, or any other — except for brief quotations in critical reviews or articles, without the prior permission of the author.

To contact the authors:
Wes Dupin: wes.dupin@daybreak.tv
Tim Way: tim.way@daybreak.tv

Cover design: Jeff Gifford and Mark Courtney
Interior design: Frank Gutbrod

Printed in the United States of America by Wesleyan Publishing House

# Contents

Forward ..................................................................................6
Dedication ...............................................................................7
Meet the Authors ....................................................................8
Introduction ..........................................................................11
Chapter 1: The History and Effects of Evangelism in
America ...............................................................17
Chapter 2: History of Evangelism in the Wesleyan
Church ................................................................35
Chapter 3: Analysis of Evangelism ........................................75
Chapter 4: Early Evangelism Pioneers ..................................87
Chapter 5: Evangelism Giants, 20th and 21st Century ...... 123
Chapter 6: Categories of Approved Evangelists within the
Wesleyan Church ............................................. 145
Chapter 7: Evangelism Training ........................................ 149
Chapter 8: Best Evangelism Resources ............................. 175
Chapter 9: Evangelism Awards .......................................... 183
Chapter 10: Evangelism Training Centers and Conferences
in the United States ......................................... 185
Chapter 11: Best Evangelism Practices:
Selected Churches ............................................ 191
Chapter 12: Concluding Notes from Wes: Rethinking
and Rebuilding a Culture of Evangelism ........ 223
Acknowledgements ........................................................... 229
Bibliography ...................................................................... 233

# Forward

Studying history can propel us forward into the future on a God-knowing and impactful path. Ignoring history puts us in certain peril because we are sure to miss the powerful lessons we should have learned, and commit the same mistakes repeatedly.

In *Almost Chosen*, Wes Dupin and Tim Way have given us a gift. They highlight a rich history of a Holy Spirit-led evangelistic movement. They use the past to inspire us to move forward in creative ways. I challenge you to read carefully and learn from those who have gone before you. Then, let your life and your church add a fresh new voice to the Story as you follow the Great Commission and walk with the resurrected Jesus into a world that needs His love and grace as much as any generation that has gone before us.

I know Wes and Tim personally, and I can't think of two better leaders to teach us the past and point us to the future. Their commitment to the Gospel and the evangelization of the world can be seen in how they live, pray, and serve the Church and engage with the world. Their words will propel you outward with a new passion to fulfill the command given by our Lord to "go and make disciples of all the nations."

Rev. Dr. Kevin Harney<br>
Founder of Organic Outreach International<br>
Author of the *Organic Outreach* trilogy of books<br>
Lead Pastor of Shoreline Community Church,<br>
Monterey, California

# Dedication

I dedicate this book to my dad and mom for all the love, prayers and guidance you have given me all my life.

I dedicate this book to Claudia, my wife, cheerleader, and greatest supporter.

I dedicate this book to my sons, Chad and Clint. You are my greatest legacy.

I dedicate this book to pastors around the world who faithfully serve in churches of all sizes. You are the true heroes of the faith.

I dedicate this book to seminary and Christian college professors who have been called to prepare the next generation of pastors, evangelists and leaders.

I dedicate this book to evangelists who preach the Gospel and call people to a relationship with God through Christ.

Finally, I dedicate this book to the staff and many volunteers who have served with me at Daybreak Church. It has been a great adventure together. I love you deeply.

Wes Dupin
Founding Lead Pastor, Daybreak Church
Hudsonville, Michigan
April 26, 2017

# Meet the Authors

**Wes Dupin**

Wes grew up in a preacher's home. His dad, Clyde Dupin, is an interdenominational evangelist conducting crusades around the world. Wes worked closely with his dad as a crusade and program director for many years, training thousands of people to be counselors in his dad's crusades. Through this, they learned how to share their faith.

In 1989, Wes founded Daybreak Church in Hudsonville, Michigan, a suburb of Grand Rapids. He, along with his wife, Claudia, who serves as Executive Pastor, are fueled by a life-long fascination with creativity and a passion for evangelism. Wes has a vision for reaching people through visual mediums and creative expression. His passion for evangelism has taken him to many difficult spots in the world, including Iraq, Bosnia, Haiti, Nigeria, and others. Wes and Claudia love to spend time with their six grandchildren, Savannah, Claire, Henry, Charlie, Reese, and Sadie.

**Tim Way**

Tim serves on staff at Daybreak Church as the Director of Spiritual Development. He has been a small group leader for over 20 years, and was a church elder for 19. He has participated in numerous mission trips to places like Haiti, Sri Lanka, Sierra Leone and Mexico, as well as in many volunteer projects.

## Meet the Authors

Tim worked for Family Christian Stores for 29 years before retiring in 2012. Positions he held there included district manager, and as a senior buyer and Divisional Merchandise Manager for various areas within the company. Tim is an avid reader, primarily in the areas of $19^{th}$ century history, $19^{th}$ century classic English literature, biographies, philosophy and Christian living. He enjoys studying both informally and in formal classroom settings, including summer sessions at Oxford and Harvard universities.

Tim has been married to his beautiful wife, Ramona, for 48 years. Together they have three grown children and four wonderful grandchildren, Sierra, Maddie, Embree and Lily.

Dr. Clyde C. Dupin
"America's Straight-talking Evangelist with a Pastor's Heart"
Statue dedicated at Southern Wesleyan University, April 12, 2017

# Introduction

This book is written to encourage and inspire you to engage others with the Gospel message; not to make you feel guilty or condemn you. In this introduction, I want to share some stories from my dad's life, and to lay out a vision for this book. I pray you will be motivated to share your faith.

My dad, Dr. Clyde Dupin, was honored on April 12, 2017, by Southern Wesleyan University for his life and work in evangelism. As a 9-year old farm boy from Hardin County, Kentucky, my dad responded to God's calling on his life. It all started in September 1942, with a tent meeting about a mile down the road from his house. There was an air of excitement as Clyde, his mother, brother, and sister all gathered under the tent that evening to hear a young 20-year old minister, Rupert Goodman, preach a simple and direct message. Rupert's message title that night was, "Whose Side Are You On?" He asked those gathered, "Are you with Jesus or against him? Do you let Jesus rule your life, or Satan? The Bible says, 'He who is not for me is against me.' Do you really let Him rule your life?" *(Hill, 1980, p. 14)*

My dad's parents were good people, but they were not Christians. They had never taught my dad to pray, but that night as he walked home he found deep within himself a hunger for God. The next night, dad returned early for the tent revival to get a good seat. Before he could sit down, a young soldier from Fort Knox named Bruce Meads put his hand on his shoulder and asked him a question: "Son, do you know Jesus Christ as your Savior? Are you a Christian?" For a moment, my dad was startled. Then he answered honestly,

"No, sir, I am not a Christian." That night my dad heard the young preacher say, "If you fear, repent, and let Christ come into your heart. Decide now and then come forward and let us pray together." *(Hill, 1980, p. 15)*

That night, without any hesitation, 9-year old Clyde Dupin stepped out and went forward. The young solder, Bruce Meads, went with him and knelt by his side. As he repented of his sins and invited Christ into his heart, my dad was born again.

Shortly following this, Bruce Meads was shipped overseas to Ireland. Later, in the Battle of Kasserene Pass in Tunisia, North Africa, Bruce was captured by the German Army and sent to a prison camp for three years as World War II raged on. From this German prison, he was allowed to write only two letters a month. Each month he would send one letter to his mother. The other he sent to Clyde Dupin, the little 9-year old boy he had helped lead to Christ, just to encourage him in his new-found faith.

In addition to Bruce Meads, there were others who mentored my dad. One was a man named Jimmy Goodman. "Brother Jimmy, as he was affectionately called, was an old white haired Nazarene minister. Many afternoons Clyde would go to his house. They would study God's Word together. Clyde was a young boy and he an old man, separated by a great span of years, but a bond of love and respect grew between them . . . [Brother Jimmy] urged him to serve God no matter the cost. Clyde told him he would! He told Brother Jimmy he was called to preach. 'There is no higher calling. Never stoop to do anything else,' he encouraged." *(Hill, 1980, p. 17)*

So, at age 10, Clyde began to preach. His first sermon was supposed to last thirty minutes, but he was through in five. But my dad practiced and improved. Soon, churches in the community would invite him to come to their church and preach. People referred to him as "The Boy Preacher," while others called him "Billy Sunday."

A critical moment in my dad's life took place following one of these special invitations to preach. After his message, one of the community ministers cornered my dad to give him some advice about his preaching and the content of his sermons. He said, "Clyde, you have a great ability and you can someday pastor large churches if you will quit this preaching on being born again. Stop preaching about a personal salvation and repenting of your sins." My dad said this advice jolted him. Here he was, just a young man, getting this kind of advice from a seasoned professional minister.

> "It was discouraging to me, just a boy in my teens, to have an older minister talk to me in this manner, but I decided that day if I never had a large church to pastor, if I never had great audiences to preach to, even if I had to preach on a street corner, I would not compromise. I would preach the Bible like it was. I determined at that early age the Bible would always be my textbook."
> *(Hill, 1980, p. 24)*

Here my dad was faced with one of the most important decisions of his young life. This influential minister tried to persuade my dad to choose a more popular, watered down message: "Don't call people out to make a decision." My dad could have very easily chosen that path, but, thankfully, he did not. He determined to never compromise.

My dad has built his life upon solid biblical principles, and his ministry continues to stand firm on this foundation even now. Dad's love for God and his Word, and his commitment to the simplicity of the Gospel message have served as the structure supporting every aspect of his evangelistic outreach.

Dad has preached face to face to over four and a half million people in more than 600 interdenominational crusades, revivals and conventions. I've been with my dad in crusades in Haiti with crowd upwards of 45,000 people in a single service. Over the years, we saw as many as 44,000 people make a decision to follow Christ in Haiti, and another 37,000 in Russia. I've always heard my dad preach a message of love, forgiveness, hope and life-changing possibilities through Jesus Christ. Now in his 80's, my dad has often been referred to as "the Billy Graham to small-town America."

Tim and I hope you gain new insights into evangelism through this book. Throughout the 20th and 21st centuries, evangelism has been delivered through one-on-one conversations, large-scale Billy Graham-style evangelistic events, Lee Strobel apologetic approaches, the invest and invite culture inspired by Andy Stanley, and multitudes of other methods. There is no "right" method. The goal is to find what works for you, and use it to bring people to Jesus. The main point of this book is to encourage and inspire you to connect with this generation right where they are with the Gospel of Christ. We hope the lessons of history, the examples of those who have gone before us, and the tools outlined here are helpful to you in your journey.

We have taken a careful look at how evangelism has impacted, specifically, the Wesleyan Church over the past century and a half. While some of our comments may seem somewhat (gently) critical, our goal is not to make a denomination look bad or to condemn methodology. Rather, our goal is to encourage people of all denominations to share their faith and bring people to Christ.

*Introduction*

If you will take the time to read this book from beginning to end, I believe, as you analyze some of these historical findings and apply biblical truth concerning evangelism in a post-church culture, you can help activate an evangelistic culture in our churches, Christian colleges, and seminaries regardless of your denomination or style of church.

*Lord, give me the courage to tell someone about You everywhere I go. May my presence in the world make a difference everyplace I inhabit. Make me salty enough that the world will call out to You. Finally, I ask you for courage and boldness to live out and communicate Your Gospel. In Jesus name, Amen.*

May God bless you as you read this book,
Wes Dupin, co-author

CHAPTER 1

# History and Effects of Evangelism on America

## Early American Religion: The Myth of Christian America

Reverend George Burroughs' ordeal was finally over. At age forty-two, he slowly climbed the rickety ladder leaning against a rough gallows just outside the village of Salem, Massachusetts. It was August 18, 1692. He had already suffered greatly through fourteen weeks in prison and a sham trial. He was ready to die. Burroughs, a minister who had served in Salem from 1680 to 1683, had been tried and found guilty of witchcraft based on the false testimony of a group of hysterical teenage girls in an atmosphere charged with jealously, hate and suspicion. As he climbed the ladder, George Burroughs briefly hesitated; many of those gathered to watch thought he was at last going to confess his crimes. He did not. In a matter of minutes he was dead.

George Burroughs was not alone that miserable morning. Others from the community to be executed that day were John Willard, John Procter, George Jacobs, and Martha Carrier, all accused of the same crime. After the grisly hangings, the victims were buried in shallow graves — so shallow that for one of the executed "[one of] his hands and his chin, and a foot [were] left uncovered." *(Schiff, 2015, pp. 298-302)* All told, there were 19 people executed in various ways during the Salem Witch Trials, and a total of 200 accused. The accused who escaped execution did so by falsely confessing to their "crimes." Most of the accused, including Burroughs, were kept for weeks on end in dark, filthy prisons awaiting their execution or release.

This unfortunate, deadly incident in a small Massachusetts town — the colony of the "good Puritans" — is a dark blot on the religious history of the American Colonies. Yet we find that the history of religion in America is not as pristine as we have been led to believe in our grade school history books.

The image of America being settled by pious, persecuted people looking for a place to serve and worship God is largely a myth perpetuated by schoolbook images of religious Pilgrims crunching through the snow to church with their muskets and Bibles. Yes, the Plymouth Plantation Pilgrims were pious, but they were by and large the exception to the rule in early America. The truth is that America has never been a truly "Christian nation" beyond lip service by our leaders and, perhaps, wishful thinking.

There was lofty talk of religion in the planning of the colonies, but actual practice failed to live up to that image. "The religious patterns that emerged in the seventeenth-century did not conform to sweet visions of a triumphant Christian future." *(Butler, 1990, pp. 55-63)* In its first century, European religious emphasis in America declined rather than increasing. Even in Puritan Massachusetts, religion tended to be a dividing rather than unifying factor.

In Virginia, there was an ardent desire by the Virginia Company leaders to establish their colony as a religious stronghold in America. Virginia's first ministers had strong

Calvinist and even Puritan credentials. But the religious desires of the company leaders clashed with the "spiritual indifference of the fifteen-to-thirty-year-old males, notorious for their spiritual indifference." By the middle of the 17th century, Virginia was spiritually better known for "irreligion and indifference than piety." While the early ministers tried to turn things around, they largely failed, and, in the end, the colony's leadership failed the community. "Despite the nearly tenfold increase in population from four thousand colonists in 1630 to about thirty thousand colonists in 1670, the number of ministers did not increase from the five to ten men laboring there in the 1640's." Further, the ministers that did labor there were sub-par. "In 1636 John Hammond described the colony's ministers as lascivious drunks who had abandoned all vestiges of Christian discipline. As one writer of the time said, they 'babble in a Pulpet (sic), roare (sic) in a Tavern.'" *(Butler, 1990, p. 45)*

Maryland was even worse. "In Lord Baltimore's Maryland, the collusion of geography, shifting immigration and settlement patterns, and government inaction left most settlers without even the simplest rudiments of public Christian practice between 1630 and 1690." *(Butler, 1990, p. 51)*

New England was the one religious "bright spot" in the American colonies in the 17th century. On the surface, New England was a stronghold of aggressive Protestantism. Yet, even with this emphasis on religion, an undercurrent of unsettlement quickly developed, brought on by a change in social and intellectual development, and by a wave of new immigrants that imported changing values into the colony. These changes, coming within a few decades of the original settlement, imported a more European feel to New England. "They shattered the older Puritan hegemony not through a new-found atheism but through their simple indifference to the Puritan churches that had been the principle means of expressing Christian adherence in this quite remarkable society." And beyond mere indifference, the ability of the Puritan leadership to control the moral purity of the colony was soon out of their control. "Even worse than the cases of premarital sex and adultery were, according to Bradford, those of 'sodomy and buggery.'" A seventeen year old servant, Thomas Granger, "was convicted of having sexual relations with 'a mare, a cow, two goats, five sheep, two calves and a turkey.'" Granger was put to death after being forced to watch the killing of his animal paramours, all of whom were buried in a common pit. *(Philbrick, 2006, p. 186)*

Church attendance was high — at first. But there was never 100% attendance. In 1635 Boston, for example, over 50% of the town's families were a part of First Church. But by 1649, just fourteen years later, over half of Boston's men, including servants, were not a part of any church. *(Butler, 1990, p. 61)*

Further, the religious atmosphere of the colonies was rift with magic, witchcraft and the occult, much of which had been imported from Europe and was mixed in with Christian beliefs throughout much of the population in the colonies, including religious New England. *(Butler, 1990, pp. 67-88)* And much of this was fanned by the very nature of the religion of the early Puritans in America. "They tended toward fissions and factions, strong opinions, righteous indignation. Like any oppressed people, they defined themselves by what offended them, which would give New England its gritty flavor and, it has been argued, America its independence . . . God was silent and maddeningly inscrutable. To discern his will, to decode his purpose, was the lifework of a Puritan . . . One was selected before birth for salvation or damnation; to which camp did one belong? That puzzle put the Puritan on edge, inwardly focused, worrying his way through the world." *(Schiff, 2015, pp. 6, 96-97)* This made the New England community rift with suspicion, intrigue, and an atmosphere ripe for the abuses of the 1692 Salem Witch Trials. Not exactly a Promised Land.

"As the seventeenth century drew to a close, the prospects for the Christian triumph envisioned in the first decades of English colonization remained problematic. Pennsylvania struck the most positive note, at least for those who believed Quakerism was a Christian religion . . . The Carolinas outdid all the colonies in their institutional lethargy. In South Carolina, the only church buildings constructed before 1695 were for refugee Huguenots, whose French-language worship scarcely attracted English listeners . . . It is more likely that Charleston's first Anglican Church was constructed in 1698." *(Butler, 1990, pp. 63-64)*

Among many English settlers there was a concern for the spiritual well-being of their fellow colonists. But this concern did not spread much beyond their own kind. Some of this was a result of their concentration on not only prospering in the new land, but simply surviving. For the first number of decades, the English had an honest and well-deserved fear of the native Americans. At one point in the early days of Virginia, an Indian uprising wiped out 20% of the English population. But while the English had little interest in converting the Indians surrounding them, the French and Spanish Catholic settlers did, and made honest attempts to introduce Christianity to the aborigines of the continent. Father Jacques Marquette, for example, brought Catholicism to the Indians in the 1600's. "Superiors sent him to build on the work of Jogues and others at Sault Sainte Marie in Michigan, where two thousand people soon lined up for baptism. Marquette and his colleagues held back with the sacrament until they were sure that the docile natives would leave behind their [heathen] customs as they turned Christian." *(Marty, 1984, p. 101)*

## The Great Awakening and its Effects on America

In the 1730's something called the Great Awakening began to happen on both sides of the Atlantic. It started in England with John Wesley and spread to other Methodists like George Whitefield, John Nelson, and a host of others. The fire soon spread to America. "Colonists had never seen anything before like the revivalist outbreaks that swept the country in the early eighteenth century." *(Marty, 1984, p. 108)*

The Great Awakening in the mid-18th century was the start of true non-European, old-style religion in the West. Up until this point the churches in America worshiped and acted a lot like the churches in England and Europe. The government even treated churches much like the old style government sponsored religious institutions of Europe.

The effect of the Great Awakening is still being felt in America. Many of the denominations which exist in America today are a direct result of the seeds sown during the evangelistic fervor of this time. The various competing evangelists "had converted people to their Congregationalist, Presbyterian, Methodist, and Baptist beliefs. Those who, like the Episcopalians, shunned the movement were left behind." *(Marty, 1984, p. 109)* This movement even affected the later resurgence of Catholicism in America, as the priests had to somewhat learn the techniques of the Great Awakening evangelists in order to win the hearts of the Catholic migrants coming to America.

It was not just evangelists from England that were changing the religious landscape in America. Home-grown men like

Johnathan Edwards suddenly began to make an impact. In 1731, "while Edwards went about his usual business preaching the terror and mercy of God, people unaccountably began to stir. For the next two years — though some saw signs of revival as late as 1737 — people crowded the aisles and pews, converting in such numbers that ever since some observers have likened to speak of the Massachusetts Great Awakening as having 'broken out' there and then." Clearly, God was at work in America. *(Marty, 1984, p. 113)*

While there was never a time in America where the majority of citizens became true Christians, the atmosphere was definitely changing. America was becoming more religious. This changed both the established European style churches and the government of America. Preachers like Whitefield undercut the established church ministers "who preached an unknown and unfelt Christ." *(Marty, 1984, p. 119)*

## The American Revolution: Positive and Negative

The rise of new churches and denominations that were "made in America" began to erode the connection America had to the motherland. As America slowly drifted toward independence, pastors began to preach a more strident message. As war became imminent, some preachers also began to become more militant in their messages. During the French and Indian War, Samuel Davies, who was to become president of Princeton, preached that to fight the Catholic French was to fight the antichrist. *(Doyle, 2013, p. 49)*

However, at the same time the Great Awakening was taking hold, there was also a rise in deism; a watered-down belief in a general god, but not necessarily in the God of the Bible. While many intellectuals believed in what they would call the

Creator or the Almighty, they disbelieved the deity of Christ, the miracles, and the atonement of Christ for sins. These deists included many influential men who would shape our nation like George Washington, Thomas Jefferson, Benjamin Franklin and others. Most of them gave lip service to God. John Adams said this at the end of his life: "The love of God and His creation, delight, joy, triumph, exultation in my own existence . . . are religion." *(McCullough, 2001, p. 614)* And all of them were adamant of the need for freedom of religion, something for which we can be grateful. Outside the walls of the churches, however, this general acceptance of deism was prevalent throughout the new nation, as were some darker aspects of European religion such as witchcraft, magic and the occult. *(Butler, 1990, pp. 218-220)*

One of the driving religious forces toward the American Revolution was the rise of the Baptist Church, a direct result of the evangelization of the Great Awakening. The first concern of the Baptists was the salvation of souls. "But as they minded their church business, they could not avoid taking political stands as well." *(Marty, 1984, p. 150)* As the drift toward the American Revolution became stronger, the competing churches — the Baptists, Presbyterians, Methodists and others — tended to unite behind the American cause and the Revolution, despite the general deism of the revolutionary leaders. The Revolution, however, largely ended the missionary efforts of the Methodist Church in America, as John Wesley was forced to recall most of his preachers back to England for the duration of the war.

## Effects of Evangelism:
## After the Revolution to the Civil War

Following the American Revolution, the influx of Methodist and other evangelists from England was renewed, and the desire to spread the Gospel grew. John Wesley was largely forgiven for his loyalty to England during the War (Americans blamed this on his being politically naive), and the number of Methodist evangelists once again increased. Francis Asbury came from England and began to effectively evangelize large portions of the new nation. And he and others were highly successful. "Before the war there were only 4,291 Methodists in America; yet at the end of his life, Asbury counted 212,000 of them." *(Marty, 1984, p. 171)* This incremental increase in conversions was felt across the nation and in all denominations. The seeds of the Great Awakening, interrupted by the necessity of the American Revolution, began to grow exponentially into what was called the Second Great Awakening as the new nation took root. This strong growth of Christianity in America continued up to the time of the Civil War, with the result being that the America of the mid-19th century was a more generally religious nation then the America of the mid-16th to mid-17th centuries. Here is a breakout by denomination:

**Comparison of the numbers of congregations by denomination, 1780 through 1860**

| Denomination | # Congregations in 1780 | # Congregations in 1820 | # Congregations in 1860 |
|---|---|---|---|
| Baptists | 400 | 2,700 | 12,150 |
| Presbyterians | 500 | 1,700 | 6,400 |
| Methodists | 50 | 2,700 | 20,000 |

*(Butler, 1990, p. 270)*

During the same time, the older European style churches experienced growth, but did not fare as well as the Baptists, Presbyterians and Methodists.

| Denomination | # Congregations in 1780 | # Congregations in 1820 | # Congregations in 1860 |
|---|---|---|---|
| Congregationalists | 750 | 1,100 | 2,200 |
| Episcopalians | 400 | 600 | 2,100 |
| Lutherans | 225 | 800 | 2,100 |

*(Butler, 1990, p. 270)*

**Total number of Christian congregations 1780 as compared to 1820 and 1860:**

- 2,500 in 1780
- 11,000 in 1820
- 52,000 in 1860, a total growth in Christian congregations of 1,980% (compared to 1780)

*(Butler, 1990, p. 270)*

In the same years between 1780 and 1860 the US population rose from 4 million to 31 million, a 675% increase. With the growth of the number of Christian congregations at 1,980%, the increase in churches far exceeded the population growth in the United States from 1781 to the eve of the Civil War in 1860. America had, because of the evangelistic efforts of the Great Awakening and Second Great Awakening, finally become closer to being a Christian nation than even its founding fathers had imagined. *(Butler, 1990, p. 270)*

What caused this spectacular growth? Obviously, it was the work of the Holy Spirit brought on by inspired preaching. The Word caught hold in the hearts of people and transformed them into personal evangelists. This message was something the old European churches had lost along the way. John Wesley's message was marked by presenting Christianity with two inseparable qualities: holiness and happiness. This was a message that rang true with the listeners in America as well as England.

"In his *Plain Account of Christian Perfection*, Wesley defined holiness not as achieving sinless perfection but as having one's heart fully fixed on God, setting aside all other affections — 'perfect love.' His teachings . . . combined the spiritual athleticism of William Law's *Serious Call to a Devout and Holy Life*, the Moravian emphasis on felt assurance of salvation . . . and the Puritan insistence on minute examination of conscience coupled with sanctified action in all spheres of life . . . Wesley taught that True Christianity fulfilled all of a person's deepest, truest desires, making the Christian a happier, more productive person." *(Armstrong, 2008)*

This was obviously a message that America was ready to hear and grasp.

## The Civil War:
## How Evangelism Affected the Slide toward War

Richard Allen was born a slave in 1760 in Philadelphia. His father's owner sold his family to a kind farmer in Delaware named Stokley. One day one of Bishop Asbury's circuit riders galloped onto Mr. Stokley's farm and shared the Gospel to both freemen and slaves alike. After a while Richard Allen experienced a new birth through faith in Jesus Christ, and, in time, was able to become a teacher of the Gospel in his own right. As Allen grew in his faith, he also learned from the Methodist circuit rider that he should be setting goals for himself as he worked toward perfection in this life. This, in turn, gave him a desire for freedom. Eventually, Richard Allen came to terms with his owner, Mr. Stokley, and both he and his brother became free men by purchasing their freedom. Allen eventually went on to become a preacher and founded the Free African Society in Philadelphia. He also helped inspire the founding of the Methodist General Conference for free blacks, following the discipline of the Methodist Episcopal Church. *(Marty, 1984, pp. 238-239)*

Richard Allen's story, while set in the northern colonies where free black men were more common than in the deep south, is representative of how the Great Awakening began to change the thinking of a nation, particularly that of black slaves, as well as a good portion of the white population of the northern states.

The movement of the United States toward the Civil War was complex, with the seeds of the war sown well before the founding of the nation. The founding fathers realized the issue of slavery would sooner or later have to be addressed, but opted to delay the inevitable until after the nation was established before forcing the potentially catastrophic issue of emancipation upon the southern states. Among the multitude of reasons for the slide toward war, the rise of denominationalism accelerated the nation in that direction. Methodist evangelists began to increasingly preach the Gospel to the black slaves of the South, a benefit the early slaves were denied. In fact, many early slave owners believed converting slaves was neither necessary nor wise. They believed slaves were sub-human, and religion was something they did not need; and by hearing the Gospel they would become discontent. By the mid 1800's, however, many slaves had come to know Christ. This resulted in a change in the thinking of the slave population, similar to that of Richard Allen. This increased desire for freedom helped push the issue of emancipation closer to a reality. So, an effect of evangelism prior to the Civil War resulted in a greater Christianization of the slave population, changing the attitudes of the South and the nation, and further accelerating the slide toward war.

In the meantime, the Methodists and other churches in the North began to preach against slavery. Harriet Beecher Stowe, a devout Christian, wrote Uncle Tom's Cabin, which further intensified the split between the two halves of the country. In 1824 Orange Scott founded the Methodist Episcopal Church over his disagreement with the Methodist Church's reluctance to take an abolitionist stand. While none of these things directly led to the Civil War, they all increased the size of the split between the North and the South, which, along with a multitude of other issues, eventually caused the Civil War to break out. *(McLeister, 1976)*

## Post-Civil War to Today: An "Almost Chosen People"

The United States emerged from the Civil War a new nation once again. In a religious sense, however, it was not as strong as before the war. The evangelization of America did produce a more "Christian" culture; but the strength of the true Christianity of that culture can be called into question. The seeds of secularism that began to grow post-Civil War are still producing fruit in the United States, and are increasingly causing cultural shifts today. Jon Butler of Yale University made this statement in his book, *Awash in a Sea of Faith*:

> "After 1865 and especially after 1900, despite ceaseless warnings about secularization and decline, Americans increasingly turned to Christian congregations and church membership as a means of formulating and

rationalizing their own religious convictions amid the vagaries of modern life. These changes had originated in eighteenth-century developments that found renewed expressions in antebellum society and that shaped the religious choices that Lincoln himself made. But Lincoln also represented the ambivalent spiritual inclinations among American's heterodox citizens, men and women whose religious practice had been reshaped by the events of the previous three hundred years both who, in Christian terms at least, still remained an 'almost chosen people.'" *(Butler, 1990, p. 295)*

To the evangelists of the Great Awakening and the followers of Christ in America today, the words, "an almost chosen people," have a disappointing ring. True, at no point were the majority of Americans ever truly Christians; but great strides had been made toward making this a Christian nation. However, since the turn of the 21st century there seems to be, despite the proliferation of churches and great evangelists like Billy Graham and others, a slide toward secularization in America that is disturbing.

While reported church attendance obtained through polls has historically hovered around 40%, a new survey shows a different picture. A 2005 article in the *Journal for the Scientific Study of Religion* claims that actual church attendance may be even lower than was assumed. Traditional Gallop Polls, which ask those being surveyed if they had attended church in the past week, have shown church attendance to be about 40%. And this has been the basic benchmark accepted. However, a 1993 survey of Protestant congregations in an Ohio county, and Catholic congregations in 18 dioceses, painted a much different picture. This study showed overall church attendance in the 20% range for Protestants and no more than 28% for Catholics. This information was greeted with skepticism. But a follow-up poll by Gallop in 1994 using differently worded questions, with follow-up interpretative questions, reduced the previous 40% number to 30% attendance. It is believed that self-reporting (relying on the person being surveyed to provide accurate information) may not be the best way to achieve accurate results.

In 2000 and 2001 the United States Congregational Life Survey (USCLS) surveyed 417 churches and found average attendance in 2000 to be 182.7 people per church; and, in 2001, to be 194.4. Since some churches tend to over-report the current year and under-report the previous year, they took the average of the two figures and came up with average attendance of 188.5 people per church (ages 5 and older). When 188.5 is multiplied by the total number of churches in the U.S. and divided by the total U.S. population, the result is an estimated worship attendance of 22.2% of the total population for ages 5 and older. *(Kirk Hadaway, 2005)* Attendance breakouts between Mainline Protestants, Evangelicals, Catholics and others do not vary much from this figure. The chart which follows shows the number of church congregations by type.

### Estimated Number of Congregations in 2005

| | |
|---|---|
| Mainline Protestant: | 82,183 |
| Evangelical Protestant: | 178,672 |
| Catholic/Orthodox | 21,975 |
| Other Christian | 36,450 |
| Non-Christian | 11,720 |
| **Total Congregations, 2005** | **331,000** |

*(Kirk Hadaway, 2005)*

Comparing the number of churches in 1860, 2005, and 2015 to the US population, there is an interesting observation to be made from these numbers.
- In 1860 there were 52,000 churches for a nation of 32,000,000 people, or *one church for every 615 people.*
- In 2005, there were 331,000 churches serving 295,500,000 people. This is *one church for every 892 people*, and this includes non-Christian churches as well as "other Christian" churches (Mormons, etc.). However, if you remove the non-Christian churches from this mix, this number rises to *one Christian church for every 925 people.*
- In 2015 we had a population of 325,482,000 and 314,000 Christian churches (a decrease in churches from 2005), or *one Christian church for every 1,036 people.* (Kirk Hadaway, 2005) (Butler, 1990)

## Bottom line conclusion:
## We are not an over-churched nation.

The chart below shows the estimated percentage breakouts of attendance by type of Christian church. This information is from the *Journal for the Scientific Study of Religion* article of estimated church attendance.

*Percent of Estimated Church Attendance in 2005 by Type*

| Denomination | Total Avg. Weekly Attendance | Est % of Adherents who Attend |
|---|---|---|
| Mainline Protestant | 9,023,693 | 19.4% |
| Evangelical | 22,233,944 | 25.4% |
| Catholic | 17,151,932 | 25.4% |
| Other Christian | 3,568,455 | 25.2% |

*(Kirk Hadaway, 2005)*

Even if this figure is off by a margin of error of even 10% to 20%, this is still a fairly dismal picture of the condition of religion in America.

Martin E. Marty of the University of Chicago Divinity School, made this observation:

> "Any view of later modern American religion is bound to give an impression of competition and chaos. Tribes, racial and ethnic groups, peoples, movements, cults, sects, and denominations kept fighting for space in greater numbers than ever before. The Darwinian 'survival of the fittest' seemed to be the first law of church life, as competitors worked to take advantage of every new device and technique that might assure group survival and prosperity. Choices became almost infinite. German sociologist Thomas Luckmann has spoken of 'the invisible religion' as the final outcome of modernity, and such religion may in the end be the strongest force in American life. This style thrived in the world of high-rise apartments, long weekends, and airport newsstands; it was made up of clienteles and not congregations, of consumers more than converts, of do-it-yourself experimenters more than people who felt called to be judged by a living God." *(Marty, 1984, p. 475)*

His is a sad statement, but true. It is the call of the Church to make the Message clear, compelling and Spirit-driven; to take the "almost chosen people" and, with the help of God, turn them into true followers of Jesus Christ in the 21st century.

CHAPTER 2

# History of Evangelism in the Wesleyan Church

## Early Evangelism Efforts within the Wesleyan Methodist Church

One dark night in the midst of the Civil War, Micajah McPherson was violently dragged from his home. His crime: refusing to allow his son, Thomas, to be conscripted into the Confederate Army. McPherson was a leader in the Wesleyan Methodist Church in Freedom's Hill, North Carolina; a church which preached abolition in this, the heart of the antebellum south. He was dragged to a convenient tree where the mob leader said, "A knotty dogwood is good enough to hang a Wesleyan on." Someone threw a rough noose over Micajah's head and quickly raised his struggling body above the ground. His tormentors then stood back to watch him die. When he stopped struggling, Micajah was cut down and his body crumpled to the ground. As the crowd walked away someone yanked the rope from around his neck and remarked, "We need the rope to hang another Wesleyan!" Amazingly, Micajah McPherson was not dead. His wife rushed to his side, carried him home, and nursed him back to health. Rather than run away, Micajah and his family stayed on and anchored the Freedom's Hill Wesleyan Methodist Church for another thirty years. Such was the grit and determination of the early Wesleyan Church. *(Drury, 2012, pp. 46, 50-51)*

The founder of the Methodist Church was John Wesley, a tireless evangelist. The early Methodists in America who followed Wesley's leading in the 1730's, were equally passionate for souls. Francis Asbury and Thomas Coke were Methodism's first American leaders.

> "Coke's passion was missions, and his work in America was interrupted by numerous trips abroad to plant Methodist missions in foreign lands. Asbury's travels were just as extensive but all within the boundaries of America. He traveled the Eastern seaboard again and again, planting churches, shaping new converts and young congregations, and taking Christ into settings as diverse as the streets of Manhattan and the backcountry of the Carolinas. His journal records sixty-three crossings of the Appalachian or Allegheny Mountains." *(Drury, 2012, pp. 25-26)*

The eventual split between the Methodist Episcopal Church which Wesley, Asbury and Coke founded in America in the 1730's, and the resulting formation of the Wesleyan Methodist Church, came over the issue of slavery. John Wesley himself was no friend to slavery. He called American slavery the "very vilest that ever saw the sun," and early American Methodists were decidedly antislavery. *(Drury, 2012, pp. 25-26)* However, after 1824 the emphasis in the Methodist Episcopal Church became evangelizing the slave owners rather than the emancipation of the slaves. So, on November 8, 1842, three Methodist abolitionists, Orange Scott, LaRoy Sunderland and Jotam Horton, announced they were pulling out of the Methodist Episcopal Church, and did so in 1843. They were convinced it would have been a sin for them to remain in a church which, they believed, had betrayed the antislavery roots of John Wesley. *(Drury, 2012, p. 30 & 33)* Thus, antislavery became the cornerstone of the newly formed Wesleyan Methodist Church.

The leader of the group, Orange Scott, was himself brought to Christ in 1820 at a Methodist camp meeting in Barre, Vermont. He soon became a circuit riding preacher, keeping a busy schedule of meetings. At first Scott ignored the issue of slavery. "Being wholly devoted to the one idea of saving souls, I omitted to examine faithfully and critically as I should, the condition of the country in respect to great moral evils." But in 1834, he wrote an article about slavery and, through this article, became involved in the antislavery discussion. Because of the reluctance of the Methodist Episcopal Church to address the problem of slavery, Scott began to work for reform within the church, but his opponents accused him of attempting to cause a split. The result was that a number of sincere abolitionists were intimidated. When Scott finally left the Methodist Episcopal Church, the number of people who went with him was relatively small. *(McLeister, 1976, pp. 20-21)*

Orange Scott was an evangelist at heart. In 1844, he wrote, "We had a fine passage home (from the first General Conference of the Wesleyan Church in 1844), spending a Sabbath in Buffalo, where we left six Wesleyan sermons — three in the Methodist Protestant congregation, two on the wharf, among the sailors, and one in the prison. They were preached by Horton, Scott, Prindle, McKee, Knight, and Brewster. There is no Wesleyan society here. On our passage from Buffalo to Cleveland, Brother Brewster preached an excellent sermon on board the boat, and in returning, our brethren appointed us to talk to the people. The congregation was attentive, and we hope was profited." *(McLeister, 1976, p. 43)*

This decision to form an abolitionist-based church was not without its struggles. The cost was great, particularly in the South.

> "Adam Crooks . . . [a] young pastor of an abolitionist congregation in the antebellum South . . . suffered severe persecution and was forced out after four very difficult years. Still, he and his companions left behind a cluster of churches and five hundred members in North Carolina and Virginia, the spiritual ancestors of all Wesleyans in the South today . . . Crooks was dragged from his pulpit and thrown into jail for disturbing the peace with his antislavery activities . . . Others fared no better, and some much worse," as in the case of Micajah McPherson. *(Drury, 2012, pp. 46, 50-51)*

Further, the new Wesleyan Methodist denomination decided to disobey the Fugitive Slave Act, a federal law that made it a crime to help and harbor escaped slaves, even in the "free states" of the North. Slaves who were found anywhere within the United States were considered property, and had to be returned to their owner. "Publically (sic) and unapologetically, Wesleyan Methodists announced in *The True Wesleyan* [a denomination newsletter] their intentions to disobey the law." *(Drury, 2012, p. 58)*

The Wesleyan Methodists did not confine their concern for slaves to the United States. They expanded into Canada, working with escaped slaves to start churches. They also provided clothing, food, medical care, education and employment to former slaves. Those who went to Canada to carry out this work were greatly encouraged to find that the former slaves had, on their own, already started churches in the tradition of the Wesleyan Methodists. *(Drury, 2012, p. 63)*

Even though the word "evangelism" does not appear in the *Wesleyan Methodist Discipline* until 1915, as early as 1843 we find a strong statement of the burning desire within the church for the evangelization of those within the community.

> "'I charge thee before God and the Lord Jesus Christ, who shall judge the quick and the dead at His appearing, preach the word; be instant in season, out of season; reprove, rebuke, exhort, with all long suffering.' 0, brethren, if we could but set this work on foot in all our churches, and prosecute it zealously, what glory would redound to God! If the common lukewarmness (sic) were banished, and every shop, and every house, busied in speaking of the word and works of God, surely God would dwell in our habitation, and make us his delight. And this is absolutely necessary to the welfare of souls. Look round, and see how many of them are still in apparent danger of damnation. And how can you walk and talk, and be merry with such people, when you know their case? When you look them in the face, you should break forth into tears, as the prophet did when he looked upon Hazael. O, for God's sake, and the sake of poor souls, bestir ourselves, and spare no pains that may conduce to their salvation!" *(Wesleyan Methodist Connection, 1843, pp. 47-48)*

In the very First General Conference of the Wesleyan Methodist Church in 1844, a board of foreign missions was appointed. Orange Scott was named as the first treasurer.

Then, in 1845, a Wesleyan Methodist Missionary Society was established in New York City. Thus the channel was formed to facilitate the distribution of contributions to missionary endeavors. *(Caldwell, 1992, pp. 80-81)*

Another evangelistic emphasis was directed at the spiritual well-being of seamen. These men were not able to attend church much of the time, so floating chapels, called "Bethels" were anchored in various harbors to minister to them. The "Wesleyans had one [floating chapel] in service in the harbor of New York City in 1844. John Miles of New York Wesleyan Conference added a second floating Bethel in Albany in 1846." *(Caldwell, 1992, p.81)*

The Wesleyans also made inroads in both American and world missions. In the 1850's they began a ministry to Native Americans in Michigan, Minnesota, Ohio and New York. Unofficial Wesleyan Methodist missionaries traveled to Kaw Mendi, West Africa, a natural choice for the abolitionist missionaries since this is where many of the American slaves originated, and where a number of them returned after obtaining their freedom. This area later became Sierra Leone, and an official Wesleyan Methodist mission was planted there on December 11, 1885, by Rev. and Mrs. Henry W. Johnson. *(Drury, 2012, p. 63.)* Two other Wesleyan missionary pioneers were Isaac O. Lenman and Alice Heise. They married and in 1902 felt led to go to South Africa and work with the men in the gold mining compounds near Johannesburg. They worked there for 50 years, and the result of their work was the eventual establishment of 150 churches. *(Caldwell, 1992, p. 449)* While the Wesleyans did not have their own overseas missions program until after 1867, they cooperated with the established American Missionary Association. *(Caldwell, 1992, p. 85)*

Evangelism continued to be an emphasis in the Wesleyan Methodist Church. During the 19th General Counsel in 1915, there was a renewed emphasis on soul winning. The method was to issue credentials to selected and approved evangelists to work at large in the denomination. In the previous General Conference, the course of study for evangelists was increased from three years to four years in length, and the number of books to be studied was raised from nineteen to twenty-five. "The changes made in 1915, were mainly replacement of textbooks, continuing the Committee on Course of Study throughout the quadrennium, and the election of a committee to prepare uniform questions on the course of study." *(McLeister, 1976, p. 150)*

During the 27th General Conference in 1947, we see this:

> "The Church's interest in evangelism was reflected in the report of the Committee on Evangelism which recommended an 'ever-increasing evangelistic emphasis' in our local churches and educational institutions, preferably employing our own evangelists who were acquainted with and loyal to our principles and practices. Provision was also made for a course of study and conference supervision of such special evangelistic workers as singers, chalk artists, and children's workers. The General Conference also elected a committee to prepare suggestions which would serve as standards for the annual conference in appointing elders to general evangelistic work." *(McLeister, 1976, pp. 214-215)*

The evangelistic emphasis continued to be focused on sending out more professional evangelists. There was not as much of an emphasis on evangelism by the man-in-the-pew.

Along the way, frustration was expressed regarding the results of the denomination's evangelistic programs. During the 1951 28th General Conference, the President of the Wesleyan Methodist Church expressed a "deep concern over the slowness of the church to grow as revealed in a detailed study of the statistics covering the past forty years, and pleaded for greater evangelistic passion." *(McLeister, 1976, p. 225)*

In the 1950's, church extension (the planting of new churches) became a primary evangelistic emphasis of the denomination. The Wesleyan Youth played a significant role in this effort.

"One strategy used in the establishment of local churches was focusing the attention of the whole Church upon aggressive evangelistic and expansion efforts in one strategic geographic and population center each year. The value of such a procedure was confirmed by the San Antonio, Texas, crusade which was sponsored by the Wesleyan Youth in 1953 under Dr. Sheet's leadership. The work there, established about one year earlier, was given real help in accelerating its growth. Another such effort was the development at Wheaton, Illinois, which also was loyally supported by the Wesleyan Youth. The goal for the 1959 Youth Week offering was for sufficient funds to pay the salary of the pastor of this project for one year." *(McLeister, 1976, p. 374)*

By 1957, church extension had grown to the degree that Rev. Virgil A. Mitchell was hired to be head of this area for the denomination. On December 30, 1958, a church-wide Conference on Evangelism was held in Brooksville, Florida. This conference started a new era of evangelism in the Wesleyan Methodist Church. A second Conference on Evangelism was held in Indianapolis at the Claypool Hotel in January of 1963.

> "Following the shift in 1959 from a dual emphasis on home missions and church extension to a primary emphasis on church extension and evangelism, the department made use of the quadrennial themes to promote its work throughout the church. From 1959 to 1963, the theme was Operation Outreach." *(McLeister, 1976, pp. 376-377)*

At the 31st General Conference in 1963, "General Superintendent Rufus D. Reisdorph spoke on 'Revival as it relates to Evangelism,' emphasizing the proposed theme for the quadrennium 'Evangelize Now!' A huge backdrop showing the world, the cross, and the Bible kept this theme before the body." *(McLeister, 1976, p. 316)*

Finally, in 1968, at the 33rd and final General Conference of the Wesleyan Methodist Church, just before the merger with the Pilgrim Holiness Church, we see this statement:

> "The executive secretary of church extension and evangelism declared in his report that evangelism was the main thrust of the Church and it was given primary emphasis. The frequently used slogan: 'Evangelism — Our Number One Task!' represented the department's concept of the 'most important task of the Church today. To 'Evangelize Now' the Church was urged to use every possible means — revivals, personal evangelism, house-to-house counseling, etc. Church extension was described as the establishment of new churches, including the purchase of property and the enlistment of personnel to extend the Wesleyan Methodist Church." *(McLeister, 1976, p. 316)*

## Early Evangelism in the Pilgrim Holiness Church

The Pilgrim Holiness Church was founded in September of 1897 by Martin Knapp, who, like Orange Scott of the Wesleyan Methodist Church, split away from the Methodist Episcopal Church. He was soon joined by Seth Rees, a Quaker. These two, plus a small group of like-minded Christians, met in Knapp's home. In 1922 the church was renamed the Pilgrim Holiness Church. *(Plemmons, n.d.)* As with the Wesleyan Methodist Church, the Pilgrim Holiness Church also had a burning desire to evangelize the world. In the 1926 *Manual of the Pilgrim Holiness Church* it says:

> "With the coming of the Savior, the establishment of His Church and the descent of the Holy Spirit at Pentecost, a new and broader field was spread out for the operations of God's children in uniting together for mutual helpfulness, worship and service, and for the evangelization of the world. While we hold that the invisible Church is made up of its militant and triumphant branches from every clime and every creed, and that every believer in Jesus is a congregation of regenerated persons, having the form of godliness and seeking the highest possible spiritual attainments, as well as the most successful means for the salvation of souls and the uplifting of humanity in general."
> *(Counsel of the Pilgrim Holiness Church, 1922, pp. 30-31)*

The founders of the Pilgrim Holiness Church, Martin Wells Knapp (1853-1901) and Seth Cook Rees (1854-1933), were dynamic evangelism pioneers. Knapp in particular was tireless, highly innovative, and effective in his evangelism efforts. Both men had a passion for winning people to Christ, and their emphasis was both international and local. They were often quoted as saying, "Holiness that is not missionary is bogus." *(Drury, 2012, p. 105)*

Martin Knapp quickly began numerous ministries that were separate from, but complementary to, the Pilgrim Holiness denomination. Here are a few of his innovative evangelistic enterprises:

- He held meetings in an empty saloon on George Street in Cincinnati, Ohio, with two services every day of the week. In one year there were 750 converts through this ministry.
- He published *The Revivalist* newspaper.
- He founded an orphanage and a school in the hills of Kentucky.
- An annual camp meeting called Full Salvation Park became one of Knapp's projects.
- In 1900, he founded God's Bible School and Missionary Training Home in Cincinnati. The school had 75 students its first year and 150 the second. "GBS imprinted Pilgrim missionaries and pastors with boldness and creativity for the sake of the gospel." God's Bible School is still in existence and still training Christian leaders. *(Drury, 2012, pp. 105-108)*
- God's Bible School ministered to the brothels and saloons in Cincinnati.
- Knapp founded the Hope College for wayward girls.
- "When the mayor of Cincinnati refused [Knapp] permits for open-air meetings, they were held anyway as the faculty and students who were participating committed to be arrested one by one, the president [of GBS] being at the end of the line. When the city backed

down, GBS responded by increasing the locations to thirteen street corners around downtown Cincinnati." *(Drury, 2012, pp. 105-108)*
- In 1908, Knapp built a "salvation barge" to reach people living on boats in "Shantytown."
- "When new laws banned distributing circulars to advertise the 1910 camp meeting featuring GBS faculty member Oswald Chambers, the students painted ads on the tops of large umbrellas and marched down the streets of Cincinnati with open umbrellas in full sunlight." *(Drury, 2012, pp. 105-108)*
- "GBS served Thanksgiving dinner for up to thirty thousand poor children each year." *(Drury, 2012, pp. 105-108)*
- GBS started "GI's of the Cross," a traveling school to GI's returning from WW1.
- "GBS graduates have had a powerful influence on the Pilgrims and even the merged Wesleyan Church through graduates like Ruth Bowman, Wingrove Taylor, William H. Neff, David Keith, and more recently Henry Smith and Jo Anne Lyon." *(Drury, 2012, pp. 105-108)*

Seth Cook Rees was a practicing Quaker, but his tendency to act quickly when he felt the leading of God often got him into trouble with his fellow Quakers. He finally contacted Martin Knapp and joined with him in evangelistic ventures.

"Rees served as an evangelist much of the time, but from 1894-96, he served as pastor of the independent Emmanuel Church in Providence, Rhode Island. At least one thousand persons were converted during his pastorate. Besides the services at the church, the congregation maintained two missions. Rees divided his church members into six corps: The Slum Corps, the Sailor Corps, the Prison Corps, the City Mission Corp, the Hospital Corps, and the Open Air Corps. Great crowds attended the services and conversions were occurring every week. One of his reports said:

> 'What a glorious year! Hundreds of drunkards, gamblers, harlots, and common sinners, as well as mechanics, bankers, merchants and church members, have been gloriously saved . . . Many drunkards have not only been saved from rum, licentiousness and tobacco; but their bloated and diseased bodies have been healed, their faces freed from rum blossoms, and their wrecked, ruined lives made entirely new.'

But in spite of such victories, he was convinced that God was telling him that he was not getting the message out fast enough, so he went back into evangelistic work. In 1896 he contacted Knapp for the first time, in Cincinnati. The two men were immediately attracted to one another and cooperated closely from this point in their common task. It was no doubt, partially at least, through Knapp's influence that Rees published in 1897 his first book, *The Ideal Pentecostal Church*. The association of the two was limited to the five-year period of 1896-1901, being cut short by Knapp's early death, but it was very important to the future Pilgrim Holiness Church." *(Wilson E. L., 2015)*

Another key evangelist for the early Pilgrim Holiness Church was Charles Cowman, who was a Western Union executive. After coming to Christ at age 31, Charles led 75 of his fellow workers to Christ in the first six months after becoming a Christian. Charles and his wife, Lettie, later founded the Oriental Mission Society, and became missionaries to Japan in 1901. *(Drury, 2012, p. 108)*

However, not all evangelistic efforts in the Pilgrim Holiness Church were successful. In 1950, the church proposed a four-year campaign of evangelism.

> "This campaign was spelled out in detail for all Church leaders, agencies, and congregations. The resolution was voted through by the General Conference unanimously. As a beginning, the conference voted to fast and pray on Friday noon of conference week, and this was done. Following the General Conference a good deal of time and effort was put forth by the leaders of the general Church and the districts to promote this program of evangelism. There were some good results, and undoubtedly a spiritual quickening followed in many places. But the effort fell short of the high expectation. Perhaps there were too many dropouts. It was still difficult for the Church to move forward in a concerted program." *(Thomas, 1976)*

## After the Merger:
## Evangelism within the Wesleyan Church

The Wesleyan Methodist Church and the Pilgrim Holiness Church merged in 1968. In the very first *Wesleyan Church Discipline* we see evangelism of the lost as the foundation for the primary objectives of the new church:

"The ultimate objective of The Wesleyan Church is to fulfill the Great Commission of the Lord Jesus Christ by sharing with all mankind the good news and glorious experience of full salvation. To this end, The Wesleyan Church, through its General Department of Extension and Evangelism and General Department of World Missions, shall endeavor:

1. To evangelize the nations of earth, seeking the salvation of the individual and the entire sanctification of believers as the primary responsibility of all missionary work.
2. To gather the converts into churches and enlist them in the work of God's kingdom.
3. To place well-qualified and Spirit-filled pastors over the churches, giving special emphasis to the training of workers and leaders for the church.
4. To share the benefits of the gospel, and to facilitate evangelistic work through specialized ministries such as medical, educational, literary, and benevolent work.
5. To promote, in accordance with Scriptural and indigenous principles, the growth and development of the churches in each field or area to a church body that is spiritually mature, well organized, financially responsible, and missionary minded, and that can assume its place in The Wesleyan Church." *(Uniting General Conference of the Wesleyan Church, 1968, p. 274)*

In the opening conference of the combined church in 1968, a banner across the front of the auditorium proclaimed, "One — That the World May Believe." *(Drury, 2012, pp. 14-15)* This became the rallying cry of the newly formed denomination.

So, from the very start the Wesleyan Church was rooted in a desire to evangelize the world.

## 1970's: The Decade of Evangelism

Evangelism in the days immediately following the merger of the Wesleyan Methodist Church and the Pilgrim Holiness Church was primarily accomplished the old-fashioned way; by holding revival services and camp meetings, and giving altar calls at the end of a church service. By the end of the 1970's, however, evangelism would include many other methods that eventually "competed with and even displaced the traditional methods . . . Increasingly, personal evangelism became the more popular method. Bill Bright's, *The Four Spiritual Laws*, swept across the church after Campus Crusade's Explo '72 was held in the Cotton Bowl, an event dubbed the 'Christian Woodstock.' In Dallas that week, 100,000 young people learned methods of personal evangelism and brought them back to their home churches and campuses. Wesleyans reluctant to use Bill Bright's tract could use their own denomination's version of the four laws called, *Have You Heard Today's Good News?* or the youth department's version resembling a credit card, '*Give the Master Charge of Your Life.*'" *(Drury, 2012, p. 231)*

The newly formed Wesleyan denomination held its first Conference on Evangelism in January, 1970. This meeting launched what would later be called the Decade of Evangelism. The thinking at this time was still much in the theme of the time-honored method of evangelism, which was the local church bringing in an outside professional evangelist and holding revival meetings. We see this from the notes of a seminar at the 1970 Conference on Evangelism: "When we consider the pastor and evangelist as a team the relationship begins with the calling of the evangelist. We assume that the church and the pastor have been praying concerning the individual the Lord would use to promote revival . . . In preparation for the revival there needs to be a projecting of the evangelist or a selling him to the church and community." *(Scott, 1970, pp. 1-2)*

One of the recommendations that came out of the January, 1970 Conference on Evangelism was the formation of a Findings Committee. This Committee was tasked with developing better ways to equip the denomination to spread the Gospel. They wasted no time. The Findings Committee met at the Indianapolis, Indiana, Airport Holiday Inn, January 13 and 14, 1970. Their work laid the foundation for the denomination's evangelism push for the entire decade.

In the Findings Committee's opening devotions, H. K. Sheets said, "We must have more than humanly devised mechanics. We must have a peculiar sense of His presence and blessing. We must challenge our people to the sacrifice, the obedience, that will bring blessing . . . now part of our task is communicating the sense of divine leadership to the church at large." *(Findings Committee, Second Session, 1970, p. 1)* Later, in the Personal Reports portion of this opening session, several of the committee members indicated how their hearts had been stirred at the Conference on Evangelism in Cincinnati, and how their personal evangelism efforts had increased. Ronald Brannon said that he had returned home from Cincinnati with his "heart aflame," and the effects of the conference were felt throughout his district. One pastor was quitting his job in order to "concentrate on pastoral evangelism. Another was changing Youth Week plans, obtaining a store front, going all out to win teens in a county-seat . . . J. L. Clark declared that Cincinnati had given him new hope. The merging General Conference had warmed to the declaration, 'Evangelism is the Answer' . . . Cincinnati shows we want to evangelize. We must now present our new program as God's plan." Lee Haines confessed to his own inadequacy in regard to evangelism and his personal struggles with prejudice toward some evangelism methods. *(Findings Committee, Second Session, 1970, p. 2)*

The Findings Committee determined that the theme for the evangelism push would be Communicating Christ in the 70's. They defined evangelism as "the fervent communication of Christ by every Christian at every opportunity to every person, so that each who will may know Him as Savior and Lord." They decided that "what was needed was a book with a total program." They also determined that what was needed was a mindset to move out of the middle class to evangelize both the upper and lower classes of people to "assist in the evangelization of our youth in our institutions of higher learning; promote home Bible classes; personal evangelism training in our schools; pioneering new churches." *(Findings Committee, Second Session, 1970)*

In the end, they decided to use J. B. Phillips' translation of the book of Acts, titled, *Young Church in Action*, printed in a special paperback edition, with a print run of up to 250,000 copies. This scripture portion would be used as a tool to evangelize and to appeal to the youth in the church. A study guide would be developed to accompany it. They decided to kick off the campaign with a 100-day thrust from September through December of 1970. Churches would be encouraged to use the book, *Can Dry Bones Live Again* for Wednesday evening teaching, and *Young Church in Action* for Sunday morning sermons. Finally, a twelve month plan for evangelism throughout 1971 was developed with each month having a different emphasis. The plan was presented as follows:

- January, 1971: Person to Person Evangelism
  - Telephone evangelism
  - Door-to-Door witnessing
  - Survey-canvas
  - Training lay-workers
- February, 1971: Literature Evangelism
  - Direct mail
  - Advertising
  - Bible distribution
  - Gospel tracts
- March, 1971: Small Group Evangelism
  - Coffee club meetings
  - Home Bible classes
  - Senior citizen and child evangelism
  - High school Bible clubs
  - Mobile home park chaplaincy
  - Extension classes, etc.
- April, 1971: Sanctuary Evangelism
  - Regular and evangelistic services
  - Musical programs
  - Children's and youth programs
  - Special day participation programs
  - Baptismal service
  - Special invitations to non-Christians to visit church
- May, 1971: Family Evangelism
  - TV evangelism
  - Family worship times
  - Evangelism of relatives
- June, 1971: Special Methods Evangelism
  - Ghetto evangelism
  - Dial-a-prayer
  - Billboards

- Street meetings
- Shopping center evangelism
- Music
- July, 1971: Recreational Evangelism
  - Exhibits
  - Fairs
  - Parks
  - Athletic events
  - Coffee houses
  - Camping (family, youth, children)
  - Retreats
- August, 1971: Special Groups Evangelism
  - Migrant workers
  - Braille
  - Deaf
  - Minority
  - International students
  - Armed forces
- September, 1971: Community Involvement Evangelism
  - Boys' Club
  - Police and fire
  - Bible marathon reading
  - Unions
  - PTA
  - Civil defense
  - National guard
- October, 1971: Mass Evangelism
  - Camp meetings
  - Films
  - Mass media
  - Cooperative evangelism with other churches

- November, 1971: Institutional Evangelism
  - Factory
  - Nursing home
  - Jail
  - Hospital
- December, 1971: Social Service Evangelism
  - Unwed mothers
  - Adoption services
  - Drug addicts
  - Rescue missions
  - Juvenile court
  - Welfare agencies
  - Counseling agencies
  - Clinics, etc.

The idea was to not make each month a stand-alone, do-it-and-done approach, but to build consecutively month on month throughout the year. *(Findings Committee, Second Session, 1970)*

The Findings Committee met again February 5-7, 1970, to report on approvals and finalize their plans for the 100-day initial thrust and the year-long program starting in 1971. One interesting statement is found in the notes of that meeting: "It was agreed to suggest to the General Superintendents and Executive Director of Evangelism that we have started the program, and that other committees and writers can be appointed for the rest of the decade." *(Minutes of the Findings Committee, February 5-7, 1970, p. 10)* While not likely their intent, this statement in a way almost implies, "We've completed our job, and we are done."

Some of the material rolled out by the Findings Committee was very formulistic, indicative of the evangelistic approach of the day. For example, one teaching-tool, complete with hand drawn stick figures, gives these instructions to Wesleyan pastors:

1. "Teach them to go prepared. Bathe every visit in prayer. If they are too late to pray they are too late anyway."
2. Teach them to work with the Holy Spirit.
3. Teach them to proceed politely. This is followed by some suggestions:
   a. Teach them to set the host at ease. If the host is embarrassed by the appearance of their house, just help them laugh it off.
   b. Find something to admire and comment on in the house: a picture, furniture, etc.
   c. Establish a common interest by asking about work, etc.
   d. Avoid discussing church membership.
   e. Come to the point of the visit, but don't hurry.
4. Teach them to present Christ positively. This is followed by a six-step outline.
   Step 1: Ask them if they have thought about spiritual things lately.
   Step 2: Ask them, "What is a person's greatest spiritual need?"
   Step 3: Ask for permission to share the way to eternal life, or ask if they have heard of the steps to peace with God.
   Step 4: Ask them what they think a Christian is; or ask them if they were to stand before God and he would ask "Why should I receive you into my Heaven?" what they would say.
   Step 5: Tell them they are about to hear good news.
   Step 6: Explain the four spiritual laws and appropriate scriptures from Romans
5. Teach them to draw the net purposefully. This part had seven steps:

Step 1: Ask them if what has been shared makes sense.
Step 2: Ask them if they would like to receive Christ and eternal life.
Step 3: Explain what following Jesus really means.
Step 4: Assuming a positive response, pray with them.
Step 5: Ask them if they really believe what they have prayed.
Step 6: Encourage them to tell others what they have done.
Step 7: Follow up with them. *(Planning Guide: 100 Days, 1970)*

In the 1970's, the Wesleyan Church also implemented another new program for evangelism. John Maxwell was a bright young pastor in Ohio who was doing evangelism in a different manner.

"After hearing [John Maxwell] speak on evangelism, Wesleyan Director of Evangelism Joe Sawyer decided that every Wesleyan leader should hear him as well. He launched Evangelism Principles in Action. This was a district-by-district tour of day-long Saturday conferences featuring Maxwell . . . The seminars were electrifying as they ranged from low comedy to high drama. Thousands of pastors and key laypersons attended these Wesleyan conferences. The event became not only a missional turning point for many churches but a time of spiritual renewal for many participants . . . Maxwell also provided resources for local church evangelism [called] GRADE; (Growth Resulting After Discipleship, and Evangelism) was the personal evangelism program Maxwell designed for his own Ohio church. . . . The genius of the program was that everyone had a role related to either doing evangelism or supporting it... Not all Wesleyan churches embraced the GRADE phenomenon, of course, and not all leaders applauded Maxwell's celebrity . . . But many who followed his evangelistic designs saw significant growth as a result. To his supporters, John Maxwell himself became a new kind of Wesleyan hero — a local church pastor-hero." *(Drury, 2012, pp. 233-234)*

"Methods of evangelism were changing in the 1970's. Even churches that resisted Maxwell's approach saw things change anyway. Unbelievers were less likely to attend camp meetings, leaving camps to focus more on building up Christians. Local revivals lost some of the appeal as well and were gradually shortened from ten days to eight (Sunday through Sunday) and finally to an extended weekend. Evangelistic speakers and song evangelists had a harder time filling their annual slate of meetings, and their number dwindled. Local churches increasingly used their own musicians for music and invited neighboring pastors to speak at their weekend meetings... If unbelievers were attending church at all, they were attending on Sunday mornings. As a result, morning services became more entry level and seeker sensitive. By the close of the decade, personal evangelism was a dominant theme for Wesleyans. Well into the 1980's, Wesleyans continued to make evangelism central, especially through youth conventions like PACE '86. The goal was the same — getting lost people saved — but the methods were changing." *(Drury, 2012, pp. 233-234)*

During the 1970's, the numbers of Wesleyan Youth began to increase within local churches. In December, 1974, 4,300 teens and leaders descended on the St. Louis Youth Convention. This was more than twice the number anticipated. They took back home an evangelistic fervor. In the mid-1970's there were just a handful of Wesleyan youth pastors in the denomination, of which the popular Jimmy Johnson from Skyline Wesleyan Church was one of the most outstanding. By the end of the 1970's the denomination had hundreds of youth pastors nationwide. *(Drury, 2012, p. 236)*

In the early part of the 1970's there was definitely a great evangelistic fervor. The question is, was it successful? The answer is both yes and no. At the time of the merger in 1968, Sunday morning attendance in the new denomination was 109,392. In 1970, attendance actually dropped by almost 6,000 people, to 103,534, but then jumped back up in 1971, the year of the big push, to 110,579. 1972 through 1974 saw steady increases with Sunday morning attendance of 111,686, 115,687, and 121,547 respectively. By 1976, Sunday morning attendance had grown an impressive 18.92%, to 130,089, as compared to the time of the merger. *(McClung) (Drury, 2012, pp. 286-287)*

But what seemed to be missing in the evangelistic push of the 1970's was building relationships with sinners, and then naturally moving them toward the Gospel. The approach devised seemed to use more of a salesman tactic — almost an arms-length "shotgun" approach — the long-term effectiveness of which may be called into question.

## 1980's: The Church Growth Movement

The evangelism efforts in the early years of the Wesleyan Denomination were basically successful, but then slowed down. In the 1980's, the emphasis was more on church planting and church growth than personal evangelism; not that the need for evangelism was discounted or debated by the denomination. Yet, as one reads the General Conference notes of the 1980's and the 1990's, there does not appear to be the red hot fire for evangelism that was evident in 1968 and the early 1970's.

During the early 1970's, with the momentum of the 1971 evangelism push and the additional use of Maxwell's GRADE program, conversions had climbed to an impressive 23,365 per year by 1976. Unfortunately, the rate of conversions following this intense push fell off precipitously, falling to only 19,244 in 1979. The 1976 rate of annual conversions was not equaled or surpassed again until twenty-three years later in 1999. The lowest year for conversions was in 1989 with only 17,886 reported. *(Drury, 2012, pp. 294-295)* Was the evangelism emphasis of the early 1970's merely a fad? *(For a more complete analysis of church growth in the Wesleyan Denomination, see Chapter 3.)*

In Robert Black and Keith Drury's book, *The Story of the Wesleyan Church*, we find this interesting statement:

> "The emphasis on evangelism in the 1970's morphed into the church growth movement of the 1980's and became an interdenominational craze among evangelicals. Counting conversions was increasingly replaced by counting attendance. Conversions were still the ultimate goal but not the measure of success. The church growth movement suggested that a person who read the prayer at the back of the tract but never showed up at church didn't count, at least for any practical purposes. Consequently, the numbers that counted became attendance, membership, and giving."
> *(Drury, 2012, p. 248)*

There is some truth to their statement, "a person who read the prayer at the back of the tract but never showed up at church didn't count." However, the figures tell a slightly different story; revealing that discounting the results of the 1971 evangelism push may be a mistake. From 1979 to 1989, attendance climbed from 129,138 to 141,879, an increase of only 9.87%. This can be compared to an 18.9% growth rate in just the first eight years of the denomination's history. In the same decade (1979 to 1989), the number of Wesleyan churches dropped from 1,791 to 1,725, a decrease of 3.68%; but average Sunday attendance per church rose from 72 in 1979 to 82 in 1989, an increase of 13.89%. But at the same time, the average conversions per churched dropped from 11 per year in 1979 to only 9.7 per year, per church in 1989. So, while the attendance per church climbed, conversions per church dropped, as did the total number of churches. The years of lowest conversions were 1985 through 1989, with 1988 being the lowest to date in the history of the denomination with only 16,770 conversions, followed closely in 1989 with only 16,960. This can be compared to the best year of the previous decade, 1976, with 12.8 conversions per church, or a total of 23,365.

While the goal to evangelize our nation and the world was certainly a key desire in the 1980's, evangelism in the new decade did not receive the intense focus it had in the early part of the 1970's. The discussion became primarily centered on planting new churches (certainly an important goal) and church growth, and not the programs of one-to-one evangelism promoted in the previous decade. In the 1984 General Conference Minutes we see this statement:

> "We entered the new quadrennium determined to face up to the tough issues confronting us. There had been

gradual decline in the number of churches in the North American General Conference since 1968 due, in part, to merging local congregations. Expanding our base of operation was essential to sustain the membership growth pattern we were experiencing. The general superintendents called together each district and assistant superintendent of the North American General Conference for a meeting in Marion, October 27-29, 1980, for a three-day study and planning conference devoted to a church-planting thrust for the decade of the 80s. A spirit of camp meeting fervency and the sense of the Holy Spirit's assistance in breaking the stagnation barrier in church planting marked the conference from the beginning to the close. 'Think -Talk -Pray -Church Planting' became the rallying call for this Great Commission responsibility. The efforts are already bearing fruit with long-range prospects even brighter. The trend of closing more churches than planted was reversed. There were 86 churches begun and 78 closed during the quadrennium. The district boards of administration were charged with the responsibility to develop goals for church planting, numerical advancement, and spiritual ministries.

The general superintendents two years later — October 25-27, 1982 — met with the district superintendents in Indianapolis. Twentieth Anniversary goals were recommended for adoption by each district conference to be achieved by the date of the 1988 General Conference. The district conferences subsequently adopted the following goals: to plant 186 churches, gain 29,772 members, increase Sunday morning attendance by 43,146, and add 6,670 conversions over the present number. These five-year primary and support goals are basic to every phase of our Church life. We are below our target for the first year on most of these objectives. The general superintendents do not believe they are too high. The achievements are too low. The task is unfinished. The quadrennium ahead is decisive. We must accelerate our church-planting efforts and challenge more of our people to become actively involved in every phase of evangelism, discipleship, worship, edification, fellowship, and stewardship." *(Mitchell, 1984, pp. 224-225)*

So, while personal evangelism was not forgotten, the primary goal was church planting. In this same General Conference there was a report of significant numbers of conversions (104,830 in four years) and the continuation of the Maxwell GRADE evangelism program started in the 1970's. *(Sawyer, 1984, p. 311)*

## Evangelism in the 1990's

Church growth and church planting continued to be the primary emphasis of the denomination going into the 1990's. In the 1996 General Conference Minutes, the General Director of Evangelism and Church Growth spent three pages discussing church planting goals and methods. Compared to this, there was one paragraph on page 292 describing a personal evangelism plan called *Commission Possible*. Here is what that paragraph said:

> "Tim Howard, a lay member of the Moline Wesleyan Church, Moline, Illinois, wrote these materials. Using a cassette witnessing program with training materials,

it enables the shyest of persons to share their faith and lead a person to saving faith In Jesus Christ. This department, in cooperation with Church Growth Institute, published *Commission Possible* for national use." *(Mull, 1996, p. 292)*

Additionally, the minutes stated that the Counsel on Evangelism met twice prior to the General Conference. The General Director's report ended by saying, "A call to prayer continues to dominate the department's ministries. Out of that ministry will flow revival, evangelism, discipleship and church planting. Also, church planting continues to be a strong focal point, since new churches by nature spur evangelism, discipleship, and revitalization...Genuine evangelism, followed by faithful discipleship training will alleviate most of our perceived and real problems." *(Mull, 1996, p. 295)*

Beyond the brief mention of the *Commission Possible* materials, there were no personal evangelism materials or programs presented or proposed. Nor was there an emphasis on evangelism in the Pastoral Letter portion of the Counsel Journal.

Pointing out the emphasis on church planting and church growth vs. personal evangelism in the 1990's is not meant as a criticism. Both elements, church planting and evangelism, are vitally important to the furtherance of the Kingdom of God. The missing element was a renewed and intense focus on personal one-on-one evangelism.

## Renewed Evangelism Emphasis in the New Century

By the end of the decade of 2000 through 2010, there seemed to be a shift in the tone of the General Conference toward personal evangelism. Phil Stevenson, Director of Evangelism and Church Growth, begins his report to the Conference in 2008 by stating, "Say if often! Keep it simple! Make it burn!" *(Stevenson, 2008, p. 245)* This statement has more of the ring of the 1968 Conference and the early 1970's.

Stevenson goes on to give this mission statement for his department:

> "The Department of Evangelism & Church Growth exists to equip and empower The Wesleyan Church to become a missional movement through multiplying believers, leaders and churches in order to fulfill the Great Commission in the spirit of the Great Commandment." *(Stevenson, 2008, p. 245)*

Couple Phil Stevenson's strong statement with the department's Core Values, and a renewed vision for evangelism seems to have emerged. Here are the stated core values Stevenson presented:

- Conversion/baptism growth is our ultimate objective; (10% conversion of Sunday AM Attendance/50% Baptized of Salvations reported);
- The purpose of church health is to become a missional force resulting in the multiplication of believers, leaders and churches;
- Every believer, every leader, every church is capable of participating in the missional movement;
- Ministry happens in partnership with districts.

This is certainly a stronger, more clarion call to evangelism than was presented by the Wesleyan Denomination in the 1990's.

Mr. Stevenson then goes on to outline goals for his department, which included salvation goals by year, baptism goals by year, the number of churches planting new churches each year, and the total number of churches to be planted by year. He clearly and correctly stated that there will never be a genuine missional movement unless it is driven by the local church. He said the "1,700 plus established churches are the lifeblood of an effective missional multiplication movement. We need churches that are willing to make evangelism and discipleship a priority. We need churches that are willing to look outward and be the representative of Jesus in their communities." *(Stevenson, 2008, p. 247)*

Stevenson also provided resources to the churches. By 2008 there were three written resources already in production which had been distributed to all Wesleyan churches. These were *Five Things Anyone Can do to Introduce Others to Jesus* (Personal Evangelism), *Five Things Anyone Can do to Lead Effectively* (Leadership), *Five Things Anyone Can do to Help Grow their Church* (Church Growth). And then in the summer of 2008 he rolled out "the fourth book in this series: *Five Things Anyone Can do to Help Start a New Church.*" *(Stevenson, 2008, p. 247)*

In the Pastoral Letter to the denomination at the 2008 General Conference there was another clear call for Wesleyans to become personal evangelists; much stronger than what was stated in pastoral letters to the General Conferences of the 1990's.

> "How then shall we witness? We witness by our stand, by the convictions we hold, by the attitudes we display, by the high sense of duty that moves us, and by the thousand little acts of love, mercy, and compassion of every day. These are the magnets by which people are

drawn to the Savior. Hear this word — life witness is not evangelism; it is pre-evangelism. Our Christian living will produce admiring observers; it will make people receptive to the gospel; but until a personal approach is made, the most beautiful Christian life in the community and even personal acts of compassion are not evangelism in and of themselves. We should have learned before now that Christianity cannot be radiated. Christianity is not only an attitude and a spirit, it is a body of truth. Christian attitudes have support only when those truths about God and His Son have been spoken and accepted. Knowledge of the truth can no more be radiated than a knowledge of arithmetic. Our witness must be definite. Evangelism involves the old necessity, which, hopefully, we will rediscover. It's called confrontation. Evangelism is personal. It cannot be addressed — to whom it may concern. We witness not only by our stand, but also by our speech. The Church speaks through official pronouncements, through church resolutions, memorials, manuals, and the Book of Discipline. But, if we are really to impact our culture for Christ, we need far more than that. Evangelism requires a host of Wesleyans in every walk of life—schools, neighborhoods, factories, and offices—who are so full of the love, power, and passion of Christ that they do not simply live a beautiful life or give bountifully to Christian enterprises, but they talk about their Savior. This will happen if we are a people overflowing with the Spirit. One wise leader said, 'The depth of an experience with Christ may be measured by our inability to keep still about Him.' That statement is more than interesting, it is convicting. The mission of the church is to evangelize the lost. This has always been our mission. We have a Christ to talk about. As a part of the holiness movement, we must not lose sight of who we are and what we are about. We are about saving souls because we believe in an unlimited atonement, that — whosoever will may come." *(Wilson E. L., 2008, p. 185)*

The effects of this renewed call to personal evangelism seemed to have a positive effect. Conversions in 2009 rose to 23,378, a 7.66% increase from 2008. Then, in 2010, conversions took another jump to 26,697, an incredible 14.2% increase.

The Department of Evangelism and Church Growth was in a state of flux during the 2012 General Conference, with several key staff members recently departed and an interim director at the helm. Thus, there was not as strong of a call to personal evangelism in the 2012 *Conference Journal* as noted in the 2008 *Conference Journal*. However, the momentum from 2008 continued, with good increases year upon year beginning in 2009. *(Pence, 2012, pp. 223-224)*

Yet, despite this improved picture, more work is needed. Since conversion records were first collected in 1974, the year 2014 was the best with an average of 20.4 conversions per year per church. While this may look impressive, what must be kept in mind is that church size since 1974 has increased 112.12%, yet the number of conversions per church has increased only 61.9%, a 51 point spread. So, the number of conversions has not kept up with church attendance. *(McClung) (See Chapter 3 for more complete information on attendance, conversions and numbers of churches.)*

## Summary

While some may be tempted to blame the denomination for the inconsistent rate of conversions, that is not necessarily the direction to look. In a doctoral dissertation titled *Evangelism Strategies for Reaching Pre-Christians in Upstate New York*, author Donald Lain points more directly to the local church. While it is true that the denominational headquarters may set the tone and drive the emphasis, the local church pastor is the driving force behind evangelism in the community. Lain cited the Barna Group:

> "Two factors are critical if the early twenty-first century church is to succeed in becoming apostolic. The first is the leadership factor. Sadly, the Barna Group discovered that less than half of all senior pastors believe they are effective in leading their churches evangelistically, less than 25 percent describe their churches as evangelistic, and senior pastors average less than two hours per week in evangelistic activities . . . In a list of sixteen factors that hinder a church's evangelistic efforts, Barna includes these: (1) 'not enough strong leadership by the pastor in evangelism,' (2) 'the absence of a strategic plan for outreach,' and (3) 'no accountability for meeting evangelistic goals and standards.'" *(Lain, 2009, p. 72)*

Lain went on to give five factors that determine, from his research, how the senior pastor's leadership in the area of evangelism is important.

1. "The senior pastor determined that reaching the unchurched was central to the church's vision." He said that his research through interviews with successful Wesleyan pastors and other research showed that, while pastoral charisma is not necessary, "the pastor's attitude toward reaching the unchurched is the most critical component."

2. "[T]he senior pastor understood and shaped the biblical and theological mandate of mission."
3. "[T]he senior pastor was the primary motivation for mission."
4. "[T]he senior pastor understood the need for cultural understanding if the mission was to be accomplished."
5. "[T]he senior pastor led in designing specific methods for reaching the unchurched. The senior pastor led in shaping both internal and external ministries."

*(Lain, 2009, pp. 119-122)*

Lain also included several factors that are common of evangelistically successful churches. These factors are:

1. The laity of the church are prepared and equipped by the senior pastor for relational evangelism. "This preparation helped laity to share with non-Christians and give a credible witness through the quality of their lifestyles."
2. The laity and the senior pastor together "infiltrate . . . the community through relational and compassionate ministries."
3. The laity invite their non-Christian friends and neighbors to attend the church.
4. The church presents culturally relevant Sunday services that make the unchurched feel comfortable. This includes understanding the importance of "developing needs-based and/or compassionate ministries."

*(Lain, 2009, p. 123 & 128)*

While all three churches Lain studied were Wesleyan by denomination, each pastor decided to give a greater emphasis to local mission than to denominational initiatives and measures of success. These "three pastors [all] agreed on the value of belonging to a denomination, especially in regard to shared theology and collaborative efforts. They also agreed that denomination participation had some obstacles that could stifle a church's effectiveness. All three clearly decided that the local church, local measures of success, and local initiatives must always supersede district or general denominational measures of success or ministerial initiatives." This decision occasionally created negative feelings between the denomination and the pastor, but they determined to put growing their church ahead of denominational priorities. "Each pastor identified themselves as entrepreneurial, occasionally at the expense of denominational affirmation." *(Lain, 2009, p. 130)*

In retrospect, the Wesleyan Church's evangelistic efforts of the 1970's, while successful, may have lacked originality. One writer, Ken Schenck, a professor of New Testament at Indiana Wesleyan University, had this to say about his recollection of that time:

> "It is interesting to watch how the Wesleyan Church rode the waves of American evangelical culture in the last decades of the twentieth century. So in the 70s we did door to door evangelism like everyone else. Then we would continue with church growth in the next decade and eventually leadership development. Of course there's nothing wrong with any of these. It just seems that we have mostly been a follower denomination rather than one that leads the way.
>
> I was only a child but those days of the *Four Spiritual Laws* and *Evangelism Explosion* made an impression on me. After all, Dr. D. James Kennedy's

church was in my home town of Fort Lauderdale, Florida. I remember going to hear John Maxwell's 'Evangelism Principles in Action' for the Florida district. I still remember him talking about how much easier it was to say 'WESSS-LEYAN' than 'Church of Christ in Christian Union.' He held the attention of a kid who had trouble paying attention to anything, which was quite a feat.

My local church implemented 'GRADE' with its Andrews, Timothys, Barnabases, and Abrahams. To this day I like the pattern. The Andrews are evangelists, the Timothys are disciplers, the Barnabases encourage, and the Abrahams pray.

Still, he was part of my childhood guilt network. He made you feel guilty if you didn't witness to the person sitting next to you on the plane, the taxi cab driver, the cashier in the checkout line. It would only dawn on me a long time later that he was born to evangelize, an off the chart extrovert who could sell ice cream in a blizzard. It wasn't hard for him to talk to strangers." *(Schenck, 2012)*

In summary, the fledging Wesleyan Denomination started on a growth spurt with the "Decade of Evangelism" in the 1970's. There was a strong call to personal layman-level evangelism. In spite of its faults, and maybe associated guilt, this call to share the Gospel seemed to work. The number of conversions per year continued to be robust through 1977. The 1980's and 1990's emphasis on church planting and church growth somewhat grew the denomination numerically, but personal evangelism appeared to wane. A renewed emphasis on evangelism in the latter half of the opening decade of the

21st century, with perhaps the improved element of building genuine friendships with sinners rather than a salesman approach, seemed to spark a new resurgence; a call to spread the Good News to neighbors, friends, relatives, and coworkers. And the change in Sunday morning services in many Wesleyan churches to a needs-based, more contemporary style made the Church a more attractive and friendly place to invite sinners. The ongoing challenge is finding ways to keep the trend of the past several years alive, and not slip back into the evangelism doldrums of the 1980's.

CHAPTER 3

# Analysis of Evangelism: 1974-2014

The analysis that follows is using data supplied by the Wesleyan Church, compiled from 1968 through 2014. The raw data used is shown on pages 83 through 85 following this chapter. The data provided by the Wesleyan Church included the following information:

- The Number of Churches each year from 1968 through 2014
- The Average Sunday Attendance annually, 1968 through 2014
- Total number of Conversions by year, 1974 through 2014

From this raw data we were able to extrapolate the following information:

- Average Conversions per Church
- Average Attendance per Church
- Conversions as a ratio of Attendance

**Disclaimer on these statistics:** In reviewing these statistics we compared the conversion numbers from 1974 through 2014 to the total number of Wesleyan churches and the Average

Sunday Attendance in all Wesleyan churches. Admittedly, the problems with these statistics are numerous: 1) Conversions recorded do not necessarily mean that these people were new attendees. These may have been people coming for a while, and certainly include children and teens who have been attending perhaps their entire life. 2) A listed conversion may or may not be a genuine coming to Christ. Some of these may be spiritual "tire kickers" who quickly drift away. 3) Methods of counting conversions may have changed over the years, skewing the figures. 4) Sunday morning attendance figures may also have been gathered in different manners over the 41-years covered by these statistics, and may, in fact, have potentially been gathered in different methods from church to church. Thus, the total accuracy of both conversions and Sunday morning attendance can be somewhat questioned. This being said, however, there are some general conclusions that can be drawn from the figures.

## Nine Conclusions from the statistics

1. **1970's: Average Sunday Attendance and Conversions was positively affected by the evangelism emphasis**
   Following the merger of the Wesleyan Methodist Church and the Pilgrim Holiness Church, there was a significant emphasis on evangelism in the early 1970's, and it was largely successful. At the time of the merger in 1968, Average Sunday Attendance was 109,392. By 1976, this figure had grown to 130,089, an 18.92% increase. In 1976, conversions were at an all-time high of 23,365 for the year. Unfortunately, the rate of conversions per year following the intense evangelism push of the early 1970's fell off dramatically, and the 1976 total number of annual conversions was not

equaled or surpassed again until twenty-three years later, in 1999. The lowest year for conversions was 1989 with only 17,886 reported. In 1977, the number of conversions fell by 5.34% from 1976. In 1978 conversions precipitously fell by yet another 12.99%. Conversions rose slightly in 1979 and 1980, but then fell off sharply for the rest of the decade. *(Drury, 2012, pp. 294-295)* There are potential reasons for these decreases aside from a lack of emphasis on evangelism. For example, differences in record keeping or even in the definition of a recordable convert could have caused some of this variation. But, as also quoted in Chapter 2, another potential reason for the sharp decline in conversions is noted in the book, *The Story of the Wesleyan Church:*

> "The emphasis on evangelism in the 1970's morphed into the church growth movement of the 1980's and became an interdenominational craze among evangelicals. Counting conversions was increasingly replaced by counting attendance. Conversions were still the ultimate goal but not the measure of success. The church growth movement suggested that a person who read the prayer at the back of the tract but never showed up at church didn't count, at least for any practical purposes. Consequently, the numbers that counted became attendance, membership, and giving." *(Drury, 2012, p. 248)*

2. **1980's: Average Sunday Attendance rises, but Conversions off sharply**
   While the rate of Conversions fell during the 1980's, Average Sunday Attendance still increased slightly, going from 129,138 in 1979 to 141,879 in 1989, an increase of 9.87%, or 0.98% per year. Considering the growth

in overall US population of 9.33%, the denomination's growth was basically flat. At the same time, the number of Wesleyan churches dropped from 1,791 to 1,725, down 3.68%. Fewer churches and slightly increasing Average Sunday Attendance, resulted in a per-church Average Sunday Attendance rising from 72 per church in 1979 to 82 in 1989, an increase of 13.89%. But at the same time, Conversions per Church dropped from an average per church of 11 per year in 1979 to only 9.7 per church in 1989. So, while Attendance per Church climbed, Conversions per Church dropped, as did the total number of churches. The years of lowest total Conversions were 1985 through 1989, with 1989 being the lowest in the history of the denomination with only 16,770, followed closely in 1988 with 16,960; an Average Conversions per Church of only 9.7 per year. This can be compared to the best year of the previous decade, 1976, with 23,365 and an average of 12.8 Conversions per Church.

3. **Conversions as a ratio to Average Attendance**
Another way to look at conversions is the Ratio of Conversions to Total Attendance. In 1974 the Ratio of Conversions to Average Sunday Attendance was 18.9%, an all-time high. Compare this to 1989, the lowest Conversion year in the denomination's history, where the Conversions to Average Sunday Attendance fell to only 11.8%. By 1999 the Ratio of Conversions to Attendance had risen back up to 14.1%, but then fell to its lowest recorded level in 2008 at only 11.1%. In fact, the early years of the 21$^{st}$ Century were dismal in regard to Conversions compared to Average Sunday Attendance, with most years in the 11% to 12% range. In 2010, however, this turned around and the Ratio

of Conversions to Average Attendance rose to 13.07% and has stayed in the 13% to 14% range since. 2014 had a very respectable Ratio of Conversions to Sunday Attendance of 14.6%. So, while still not as high as in 1974, the current trend is not as bleak as it was in 2003 through 2009, and during the conversion slump of the 1980's.

4. **Effect of the decline in Conversions on Average Sunday Attendance**

   The number of conversions at times seems to affect overall Sunday attendance. In 1984 and 1985, for example, conversions fell by 3.25% and 10.14% respectively. In 1984 overall attendance also dropped for the first time in denomination history, and dropped again in 1985. These drops were very slight, but the fact is that attendance in 1983 through 1986 was virtually flat, and, at the same time, conversions were also down or flat. Again, in 1994, conversions were down 7.16% compared to 1993, and 1994's attendance was down by 1.50%. However, a decrease in conversions does not always result in a decrease in attendance. For example, in 2001 through 2003, conversions were down 6.60%, 4.93%, and 2.75% year-to-year respectively, yet attendance climbed 0.63%, 2.41%, and 1.36% during those same years. This would indicate that church growth was coming through transfers of Christians from other denominations.

5. **Average Conversions per Church 1974 compared to 2014**

   Since conversion records were first recorded in 1974, 2014 was the best year on record, with an average of 20.4 Conversions per Church for the year. This accomplishment is impressive. However, what must be noted is that while church size since 1974 has increased 112.12%, the number of Conversions per Church has increased only 61.9%, a negative 51 point spread. **The bottom line is that the number of conversions is not keeping up with the rate of church growth.** See the graph on page 83. This clearly shows the rise in Average Sunday Attendance as compared to the relatively flat rate of Conversions. *(McClung) (Drury, 2012, pp. 286-287)*

6. **Number of Wesleyan churches in 1974 compared to 2014**
   There were 1,828 Wesleyan churches in 1974. The number in 2014, 41 years later, was 1,654, a decrease of 9.5%.* This occurred despite the push in the 1980's and 1990's on church planting and growth. The number of people saved in 1974 was 22,968 compared to 33,780 in 2014, an increase of 47.1%. However, if the number of churches in 2014 had been the same as in 1974, and the number of converts per church remained the same as in 2014, the total converts in 2014 would potentially have been 37,291, or 10% more.

   *It is recognized that the 9.5% decrease in churches in not necessarily a failing of the denomination. Many of the churches closed likely needed to be closed due to underperformance, and a consolidation for efficiency of "competing" congregations of Wesleyan Methodist and Pilgrim Holiness at the time of the merger.

7. **Average Sunday Attendance in 1974 compared to 2014**
   The Average Sunday Attendance is up 47.1% in 2014 compared to 1974. While on the surface this is a sizeable increase, it amounts to an average growth of only 1.15% per year. Nor does this keep up with the population increase within the United States which has risen 49.1% the past 41 years.

8. **2013 and 2014 were excellent years for Conversion numbers**

   Definite bright spots in these figures are 2013 and 2014. While Average Sunday Attendance grew 4.03% and 3.57% respectively, Conversions grew 9.15% and 6.23%, a strong positive trend in both indicators. In these same years, Conversions grew from 17.1 per church in 2012, to 18.9 Conversions per Church in 2013, and jumped again to 20.4 in 2014. On the down side, the total number of churches declined in both 2013 and 2014, as had been the trend since 2006, with the exception of 2008 where there was an increase of three churches.

9. **Conversions are not adding proportionate numbers to Average Sunday Attendance**

   One glaring disconnect is the apparent failure to retain current attendees while adding converts. There is no year since 1974 where the number of Sunday morning attendees increased in direct proportion to the number of converts from the previous year. For example, in 1974, Average Sunday Attendance was 121,547, and 22,968 converts were reported. Average Sunday Attendance in 1975, however, was only 129,559, a net increase of 9,012 people instead of the 22,968 converts added the previous year. Another example is 1993, where Average Sunday Attendance was 153,794, and 19,947 Conversions were recorded. But the next year, 1994, Average Sunday Attendance fell to 152,663, a loss of over 1,000 people, despite almost 20,000 Conversions recorded in 1993. Where did these 20,000 people go? There are several possible reasons for this ongoing discrepancy:

- Obviously there are a number of people already attending a church who decide to follow Christ (teens, children, and adults currently attending). Thus, not all converts recorded are new people coming into the church.
- The "back door" at most churches is fairly significant. People leave to attend other churches, people get discouraged with their faith and quit attending, people move away and attend a non-Wesleyan church in another city, and the list goes on.
- Some people come into the church, make a profession of faith, but do not follow through and immediately move on. Jesus even talked about several categories of these people in his Parable of the Sower.

The point, however, is that, for whatever reasons, most conversions do not seem to result in incremental growth for the Church.

## Conclusion: We can do better

While these figures do not tell the whole story, the bottom line is that we can do better. Attendance is rising slowly, but the conversion rates compared to attendee growth is not keeping pace. This would indicate that perhaps much of the growth is coming from transfers from other denominations. Or perhaps seekers are attending, yet not becoming followers. There was, however, definite improvement in Conversions over the trend of the past in the years 2009 through 2014, with 2013 and 2014 being significant bright spots. Average Growth per Church is also increasing, as is the percent of conversions compared to average attendance. All of these are positive indicators.

*Analysis of Evangelism: 1974-2014*

**Conversions Compared to Sunday Attendance in the Wesleyan Church, 1974-2014**

## Statistics of Conversions, Number of Churches, Average Sunday Attendance. The Wesley Church, 1968-2014

| Year | Conversions | % Incr/Decr in Conversions | Number of Churches | % incr/decr in # of Churches | Average Conversions per Church | % incr/decr Average Conversions/Church | Average Sunday Attendance | Average Attendance / Church | Average % Incr/Decr per Church | Ratio of Conversions to Avg Sunday Attendance |
|---|---|---|---|---|---|---|---|---|---|---|
| 1968 | n/a | n/a | 1,989 |  | n/a | n/a | 109,392 | 55 |  | n/a |
| 1969 | n/a | n/a | 1,945 | -2.21% | n/a | n/a | 103,312* | 53 | -3.4% | n/a |
| 1970 | n/a | n/a | 1,898 | -2.42% | n/a | n/a | 103,534 | 55 | 2.7% | n/a |
| 1971 | n/a | n/a | 1,875 | -1.21% | n/a | n/a | 110,579 | 59 | 8.1% | n/a |
| 1972 | n/a | n/a | 1,857 | -0.96% | n/a | n/a | 111,686 | 60 | 2.0% | n/a |
| 1973 | n/a | n/a | 1,847 | -0.54% | n/a | n/a | 115,687 | 63 | 4.1% | n/a |
| 1974 | 22,968 |  | 1,828 | -1.03% | 12.6 |  | 121,547 | 66 | 6.2% | 18.9% |
| 1975 | 23,043 | 0.33% | 1,832 | 0.22% | 12.6 | 0.0 | 129,559 | 71 | 6.4% | 17.8% |
| 1976 | 23,365 | 1.40% | 1,820 | -0.66% | 12.8 | 0.0 | 130,089 | 71 | 1.1% | 18.0% |
| 1977 | 22,117 | -5.34% | 1,808 | -0.66% | 12.2 | -0.0 | 128,575 | 71 | -0.5% | 17.2% |
| 1978 | 19,244 | -12.99% | 1,790 | -1.00% | 10.8 | -0.1 | 129,117 | 72 | 1.4% | 14.9% |
| 1979 | 19,678 | 2.26% | 1,791 | 0.06% | 11.0 | 0.0 | 129,138 | 72 | -0.0% | 15.2% |
| 1980 | 21,125 | 7.35% | 1,785 | -0.34% | 11.8 | 0.1 | 134,817 | 76 | 4.7% | 15.7% |
| 1981 | 20,946 | -0.85% | 1,789 | 0.22% | 11.7 | -0.0 | 137,885 | 77 | 2.0% | 15.2% |
| 1982 | 19,990 | -4.56% | 1,824 | 1.96% | 11.0 | -0.1 | 137,998 | 76 | -1.8% | 14.5% |
| 1983 | 20,026 | 0.18% | 1,800 | -1.32% | 11.1 | 0.0 | 140,955 | 78 | 3.5% | 14.2% |
| 1984 | 19,375 | -3.25% | 1,730 | -3.89% | 11.2 | 0.0 | 140,800 | 81 | 3.9% | 13.8% |
| 1985 | 17,410 | -10.14% | 1,788 | 3.35% | 9.7 | -0.2 | 140,316 | 78 | -3.6% | 12.4% |
| 1986 | 17,441 | 0.18% | 1,779 | -0.50% | 9.8 | 0.0 | 140,536 | 79 | 0.7% | 12.4% |
| 1987 | 17,340 | -0.58% | 1,769 | -0.56% | 9.8 | -0.0 | 141,574 | 80 | 1.3% | 12.2% |
| 1988 | 16,960 | -2.19% | 1,746 | -1.30% | 9.7 | -0.0 | 141,553 | 81 | 1.3% | 12.0% |
| 1989 | 16,770 | -1.12% | 1,725 | -1.20% | 9.7 | 0.0 | 141,879 | 82 | 1.5% | 11.8% |

\* Worship attendance was difficult to determine in 1969. The figure of 103,312 is an estimate.

*Analysis of Evangelism: 1974-2014*

| Year | Conversions | % Incr/Decr in Conversions | Number of Churches | % incr/decr in # of Churches | Average Conversions per Church | % incr/decr Average Conversions/Church | Average Sunday Attendance | Average Attendance/Church | Average % Incr/Decr per Church | Ratio of Conversions to Avg Sunday Attendance |
|---|---|---|---|---|---|---|---|---|---|---|
| 1990 | 17,886 | 6.65% | 1,700 | -1.45% | 10.5 | 0.1 | 142,726 | 84 | 2.1% | 12.5% |
| 1991 | 19,275 | 7.77% | 1,698 | -0.12% | 11.4 | 0.1 | 146,844 | 86 | 3.0% | 13.1% |
| 1992 | 18,918 | -1.85% | 1,684 | -0.82% | 11.2 | -0.0 | 153,228 | 91 | 5.2% | 12.3% |
| 1993 | 19,947 | 5.44% | 1,665 | -1.13% | 12.0 | 0.1 | 153,794 | 92 | 1.5% | 13.0% |
| 1994 | 18,519 | -7.16% | 1,678 | 0.78% | 11.0 | -0.1 | 152,663 | 91 | -1.5% | 12.1% |
| 1995 | 18,574 | 0.30% | 1,657 | -1.25% | 11.2 | 0.0 | 155,043 | 94 | 2.8% | 12.0% |
| 1996 | 20,406 | 9.86% | 1,660 | 0.18% | 12.3 | 0.1 | 158,263 | 95 | 1.9% | 12.9% |
| 1997 | 20,755 | 1.71% | 1,660 | 0.00% | 12.5 | 0.0 | 164,582 | 99 | 4.0% | 12.6% |
| 1998 | 21,635 | 4.24% | 1,676 | 0.96% | 12.9 | 0.0 | 168,814 | 101 | 1.6% | 12.8% |
| 1999 | 24,437 | 12.95% | 1,679 | 0.18% | 14.6 | 0.1 | 172,432 | 103 | 2.0% | 14.2% |
| 2000 | 25,411 | 3.99% | 1,689 | 0.60% | 15.0 | 0.0 | 178,451 | 106 | 2.9% | 14.2% |
| 2001 | 23,733 | -6.60% | 1,703 | 0.83% | 13.9 | -0.1 | 181,069 | 106 | 0.6% | 13.1% |
| 2002 | 22,564 | -4.93% | 1,696 | -0.41% | 13.3 | -0.0 | 184,665 | 109 | 2.4% | 12.2% |
| 2003 | 21,943 | -2.75% | 1,690 | -0.35% | 13.0 | -0.0 | 186,506 | 110 | 1.4% | 11.8% |
| 2004 | 24,434 | 11.35% | 1,714 | 1.42% | 14.3 | 0.1 | 190,738 | 111 | 0.8% | 12.8% |
| 2005 | 22,346 | -8.55% | 1,731 | 0.99% | 12.9 | -0.1 | 193,868 | 112 | 0.6% | 11.5% |
| 2006 | 22,053 | -1.31% | 1,723 | -0.46% | 12.8 | -0.0 | 195,441 | 113 | 1.3% | 11.3% |
| 2007 | 22,973 | 4.17% | 1,714 | -0.52% | 13.4 | 0.0 | 195,203 | 114 | 0.4% | 11.8% |
| 2008 | 21,714 | -5.48% | 1,717 | 0.18% | 12.6 | -0.1 | 195,596 | 114 | 0.0% | 11.1% |
| 2009 | 23,378 | 7.66% | 1,716 | -0.06% | 13.6 | 0.1 | 203,076 | 118 | 3.9% | 11.5% |
| 2010 | 26,697 | 14.20% | 1,716 | 0.00% | 15.6 | 0.1 | 204,245 | 119 | 0.6% | 13.1% |
| 2011 | 27,289 | 2.22% | 1,713 | -0.17% | 15.9 | 0.0 | 208,973 | 122 | 2.5% | 13.1% |
| 2012 | 29,133 | 6.76% | 1,705 | -0.47% | 17.1 | 0.1 | 221,335 | 130 | 6.4% | 13.2% |
| 2013 | 31,798 | 9.15% | 1,686 | -1.11% | 18.9 | 0.1 | 227,692 | 135 | 4.0% | 14.0% |
| 2014 | 33,780 | 6.23% | 1,654 | -1.90% | 20.4 | 0.1 | 231,339 | 140 | 3.6% | 14.6% |

*(Drury, 2012. p. 283-285) (McClung)*

CHAPTER 4

# Early Evangelism Pioneers

**Common Characteristics of Early Evangelism Pioneers:**
As we read the biographies of early evangelism pioneers, we see some common threads in most of their lives.

1. **What was *not* common among them was their background and upbringing.**
   John and Charles Wesley were the sons of an Anglican minister, as was their mother, Susanna. George Whitefield, on the other hand, grew up in a tavern and was destined to live a life of sin until God got ahold of his life. John Nelson was a mason, and the son of a mason. Lady Huntingdon was a member of English nobility, the daughter of an Earl. As a young man, D.L. Moody was a shoe salesman and very much a rebel; so much so that he was denied church membership. So, while the early pioneers of evangelism had many similar characteristics, the one un-common characteristic was their background and upbringing.

2. **Almost all of the early evangelists were dramatically converted, some after struggling with the concept of grace for years.**
   One exception to this was Susanna Wesley. She was brought up by a conservative Anglican pastor, and seemed to have

never strayed from her early faith. However, her son, John, despite his religious upbringing, took an extended time to discover grace, not understanding it until he had traveled to America to work with the American natives.

John Nelson, as a young man, was haunted by and terrified of the thought of death and subsequent judgement. He heard John Wesley preach and fell to his knees giving his heart to Christ.

George Whitefield was destined to live a rough life, being the son of an innkeeper. He somehow got hold of a copy of Kempis' *Imitation of Christ*, which dramatically changed his life. He managed to attend Oxford on a work/study program and, while there, fell in with Wesley and the Holy Club. Despite becoming very legalistic, Whitefield eventually came to a genuine faith in Christ.

3. **All of the early evangelists faced strong, often violent, opposition, but persevered.**
Charles and John Wesley were shunned and shut out of the official Church of England and had to find makeshift places to preach and worship. After their father was placed in jail for his refusal to conform to the official church, Susanna continued to hold meetings in their home.

George Whitefield had stones, rotten food and dead cats thrown at him as he preached in America, yet he persevered and overcame, sparking a revival in the colonies.

Francis Asbury faced the threat of attack by Native Americans as he preached in the wilderness of the United States.

John Nelson faced the mockery of his friends and neighbors following his dramatic conversion.

4. **All were strongly called by God to spread the Gospel.**
   Even before John Wesley was truly a convert, he had a strong calling to spread the Gospel in America.

   George Whitefield almost immediately began to preach with dramatic results following his conversion.

   Barbara Heck had such a desire to see souls saved that she was able to compel others to share the Gospel. They said that it was a fire burning in her eyes.

5. **All of them sacrificed themselves for the cause of proclaiming the Gospel.**
   Martin Knapp so exhausted himself in his efforts to evangelize the world that he died at age 48.

   George Whitefield often said that he wanted to die while preaching or just after he preached. He almost got his wish, dying shortly after delivering a Gospel message. He was only 56 years old.

   John Nelson would work during the day as a mason and preach at night; an exhausting schedule.

6. **Their evangelism started at home and spread out from there.**
   Martin Knapp started leading services in his home town of Cincinnati. From there he moved into world-wide evangelism.

   Susanna Wesley never left England, but her influence was felt world-wide through her sons. John Wesley was truly converted only after he returned from trying to evangelize the American colonies. He then started where he was, preaching wherever he could, and then branching out world-wide.

John Nelson started in his workplace, where he began leading those around him to Christ. He was so determined to lead men to Christ that he once paid a fellow worker to go and hear John Wesley preach. The man was converted, along with his wife.

7. **The plight of the lost moved all of them emotionally. They were compelled to witness.**
George Whitefield once said that he could not help but weep when he thought that men's souls were headed for destruction.

## Early Methodist Evangelism Pioneers: 18th and 19th Century

Barbara Heck was in a holy rage. The year was 1765, and the place was colonial New York. Barbara and her husband were German immigrants who converted to Methodism in Ireland and then crossed over to America. Like many immigrants, their religion somewhat lapsed in the struggle to survive in the New World. On this particular day, Barbara walked into the house to discover her husband and other men of the community playing cards and gambling. She instantly blew up, and, in a fit of anger, snatched the cards from the hands of the astonished men and threw them in the fire. She then turned her fury on the card-players and began yelling and berating them for their sins. But she was not through. Storming out of the house Barbara rushed to the home of Philip Embury, a former Methodist preacher from Ireland who had come to their community. She demanded that he preach to them. When he hesitated, Barbara's eyes blazed fury and she got right up close, and likely with a finger in his face, said, "Philip, you must preach to us, or we shall all go to Hell together and God will require our blood at your hands!" Out-maneuvered, Embury had no choice in the presence of this determined and angry woman but to oblige. The result was an astonishing revival among the colonists that changed America.

This is just one of many stories of those responsible for the rise of the Great Awakening in America. In these stories there are numerous heroes. Here are just a few of them.

### Susanna Wesley (1669 — 1742):

Born Susanna Annesley to parents with ties to nobility. Her father attended Oxford University. He was later driven from his parish (along with 2,000 other clergymen) for his "fidelity to the dictates of conscience" in regard to opposition to the Act of Uniformity of 1662. At age 19 Susanna married Rev. Samuel Wesley, a curate of a London parish. Samuel Wesley's father and grandfather were both also driven from their parishes for refusing to obey the Uniformity Act, and his father was four times placed in prison for his beliefs.

Susanna was well educated by her parents. She had a good literary taste and exhibited solid judgement. Susanna was also very pious. She read her Bible daily and practiced prayer twice a day; an hour in the morning and an hour in the evening. She was not musical, so her sons probably acquired their ability to compose music from her father.

Her husband, Samuel, was curate of a small church in Epworth, England. He boldly denounced sin in his parish, and some came to resent him for his blunt talk. These men wounded his cattle, set his house on fire twice, shot off guns and shouted beneath his windows. They finally managed to have him arrested and thrown into prison for three months over a small debt. Susanna tried to get him to take her rings to buy his release from prison, but he refused to take them, choosing rather to remain in imprisoned.

Susanna gave birth to 19 children. Several of these died young. At one point there were 13 children alive at one time. She greatly loved her children, especially her daughters. All of them were intelligent. Some of them were witty and others were artistic. Several of her daughters were very beautiful. Susanna made her home a fun place, even introducing games of skill and chance, some of which John later banned from the Methodist churches. Education of the children was an important part of the home.

Religious training for the children began at birth. Even before they could speak, the children were taught to use sign language as a blessing. And as soon as they were able, they were taught to read the Bible, made to keep at it until they mastered the lesson perfectly. One of the girls was able to read Greek by the time she was eight years old.

Susanna was an evangelist to her neighborhood. When her husband was placed in prison and thus not able to pastor his church, she opened her home for religious services, with up to 200 people present. Susanna herself led these services, reading sermons that she was able to find. When some complained that a woman was delivering the sermons, she pointed out that the men present could not read well enough to do so.

On one occasion when those who opposed them set fire to their home, Susanna was in poor health and was not able to escape through a window. She was forced to fight her way through the flames, badly burning her hands. John would have died in this fire had not two neighbors rescued him through an upper window, one standing on the shoulders of the other to pull him to safety. In this fire they lost everything. Following it, John's father gathered his family together and said, "Come, friends, let us kneel down and thank God; He has given me all my eight children; I am rich enough." *(Withrow, 1898, pp. 25-33)*

After her husband's death, Susanna aided her sons. When many people complained of the oddness of John Wesley preaching in a field, she saw God's hand working and "stood by her son on Kennington Common as he proclaimed the Gospel to an audience of twenty thousand persons." *(Withrow, 1898, pp. 25-33)*

### *John Wesley (1703 — 1791) and Charles Wesley (1707 — 1788):*

Born 1703, John studied at Charterhouse School in London starting at age 13. At age 16 he entered Christ Church College at Oxford. He lectured in Greek at age 23, and became one of Oxford's foremost Hebrew scholars. At age 28, John founded the "Holy Club" which met to study the Greek New Testament, for self-examination, and prayer. The methodical lives of the Holy Club members caused them to be called "Methodists." Charles, his brother, was five years younger than John.

When his father died, John was offered his father's rectory at Epworth. Rather than accepting, he sailed with his brother, Charles, to America. On the ship they traveled with a group of German Moravians who greatly impressed the brothers. During a fierce storm the Moravians stayed calm, praying and singing, and were not afraid to die. This was a lesson that John and Charles had not yet learned.

The Wesley brothers worked in Georgia. Their existence was rough, living on bread and water. John often went barefoot to encourage the boys in his school to greater piety. The colonists, however, did not appreciate this type of ascetic piety, and the Wesley brothers soon found it expedient to return to England.

The interesting thing is that John had not yet had a true conversion experience. He was pious and "religious" but did not understand grace. He wrote in his journal, "I went to America to convert the Indians, but, oh! Who shall convert me? I have a fair summer religion; I can talk well, nay, and believe myself, while no danger is near; but let Death look me in the face, and my spirit is troubled, nor can I say to die is gain," He attended Moravian services in London. One night as a layman read Luther's preface to Romans, Wesley said, "I felt my heart strangely warmed. I felt I did trust in Christ and Christ alone for salvation, and an assurance was given me that He had taken away my sins, even mine, and saved me from the law of sin and death." This assurance of faith came at age 35. *(Withrow, 1898, pp. 42-53)*

After this, John preached "repentance, the remission of sins, and free salvation. Joined by his brother, Charles, and George Whitefield, he went everywhere preaching with strange power this new evangel of the grace of God." In 1739, John repurposed an old foundry in London as the first church where the people were called Methodists. It was a large building, and he could not really afford it, but he stepped out in faith. He turned part of the building into a school, another part into a book room, and a still another into a place of worship. A dispensary and an alms-house were also added in 1748. By 1743, there were 2,200 members meeting in 66 classes in the building. *(Withrow, 1898, pp. 54-57)*

At first John was against using lay-preachers, but his mother, Susanna, encouraged him to not stop them from preaching. So, John began to train and raise up lay-preachers. His mother told him, "It is the Lord. Let Him do what seemeth to Him good." *(Withrow, 1898, pp. 54-57)*

Because of the irregularities of their style, the Wesley brothers faced persecution. Charles was ejected from his church and was threatened with excommunication by the Archbishop of Canterbury. Without a church, they began to preach anywhere they could. They faced hostility from many, and physical violence was frequent. On one occasion John was rushed by an angry military officer who drew his sword and put it on John's chest. John opened his shirt and said, "I fear God and honor the King." Another time a man tried to kill him with an oak bludgeon. The man aimed at John's head, but the blows were miraculously turned aside. During one attack Wesley prayed out loud and "the ruffian who had headed the mob, a beer-garden prize fighter, was struck with awe, and turning to him, said 'Sir, I will spend my life for you; follow me, and not one soul here shall touch a hair of your head.'" *(Withrow, 1898, pp. 54-62)*

Wesley started Methodist classes. Because they were shut out of the official church, they started classes and societies everywhere. He wrote the *General Rules of the United Societies* which became a part of the constitution of the early Methodist Church. Traveling preachers went everywhere and chapels began to spring up. "John made many visits to Ireland... Sometimes he was bitterly persecuted by a Roman Catholic mob, but often he was astonished at their cordiality and goodwill. He describes them as an immeasurably loving people." *(Withrow, 1898, p. 68)*

After returning to England from America, John Wesley preached 42,400 sermons, a rate of 15 a week. His last sermon was delivered on February 22, 1791. *(Withrow, 1898, p. 81)* On John Wesley's tombstone is this statement: "I look upon all the world as my parish." Also on the tombstone is inscribed "God buries His Workmen, but Carries on His Work." Dr. Daniels said this about John Wesley: "Other heroes have earned their honors by ravaging sea and land to kill, burn and destroy: Wesley, with equal courage and equal skill, achieved his fame not by killing, but by saving men." *(Withrow, 1898, p. 90)*

John Wesley's younger brother, Charles, wrote over four-thousand hymns, of which two-thousand still remain in manuscript and six-hundred were placed into the Wesleyan hymnal. *(Withrow, 1898, p. 90)*

### *John Nelson (1707 — 1770):*

Born in 1707, John Nelson was brought up as a mason. His father was also a mason. As a boy, Nelson was "horribly terrified with the thoughts of death and judgement. After hearing John Wesley preach, he came under tremendous conviction. He fell to his knees praying three times. Finally he said, 'Lord, thy will be done; damn or save.' At that very moment he was free." *(Withrow, 1898, p. 94)*

The Sunday following his salvation, John was ordered to work at his masonry job. He refused. The master was furious, but because he respected John, he relented. From that point on, the men at his business were never again asked to work on Sundays.

John Nelson was driven to evangelism. "Such a desire for the salvation of souls now possessed him that he hired one of his fellow-workmen to hear Mr. Wesley preach, which led to his conversion and that of his wife." *(Withrow, 1898, p. 95)*

Nelson shared Christ, despite his neighbors and friends mocking him. Even his wife did not agree with him. But very soon most of his relatives became believers in Christ, and for several weeks six to seven people per week came to salvation because of his witness. People would beg him to preach to them. At one point a large group of people gathered in a field and asked him to preach. He responded by falling on his face for an hour seeking

God's guidance. Finally, he said, "Lord, I am ready to go to hell and preach to the devils if Thou require it." *(Withrow, 1898, pp. 95-96)*

John Nelson did not have an easy life. He was bi-vocational, working as a stone mason during the day, and preaching at night; an exhausting schedule. Additionally, Satan attacked Nelson and he suffered great temptation. At one point, in short order, his daughter died, his son was dying, his wife fell from a horse and was crippled, his mother was sick, and his father-in-law died. John Nelson passed away in 1770 at age 63. *(Withrow, 1898, p. 95)*

### *George Whitefield (1714 — 1770):*

Born 1714, the son of an inn keeper, George Whitefield grew up in a tavern. At age 15 he began working in the bar-keeping business. "If the Almighty had not prevented me by His grace, I had now been sitting in darkness under the shadow of death." *(Withrow, 1898, p. 117)* Whitefield managed somehow to come across a copy of Kempis' *The Imitation of Christ*, which convicted him of his sin. He soon desired to be a scholar and was allowed to attend Oxford as a servitor, doing the work of a servant for other students. He worked hard trying to earn his pardon from sin; fasting twice a week and praying throughout each day. "But, I knew no more than I was to be born a new creature in Jesus Christ than if I was never born at all." *(Withrow, 1898, p. 118)* Whitefield eventually joined Wesley's "Holy Club" and began to live by their rules; praying and fasting and working ever harder to earn salvation. "But at last he was able to lay hold of the Cross by a living faith, and the burden of his guilt rolled forever away." *(Withrow, 1898, p. 120)* This does not mean that Whitefield's life was easy. At Oxford he was persecuted by the other students for his poor clothes and his piety. He was a poor man living in a rich man's world.

After Oxford, Whitefield was ordained as a minister by the Bishop of Gloucester. Following this, he preached wherever he could. Wesley finally invited him to come to America.

"He started to Bristol to sail for America, preaching wherever he had a chance. The churches were thronged before dawn with people lighting their way with lanterns to hear him. He understood the language and the heart of the common people, and they heard him gladly. He spoke directly to their souls, which responded warmly to his appeals. On shipboard, he preached with strange power to the soldiers, sailors, emigrant — a wicked and reckless class. In Georgia, he labored zealously among the Indians as well as the white people." *(Withrow, 1898, pp. 121-122)*

In America, this poor barkeeper turned minister preached to crowds of as many as 20,000 people. He preached to the miners, and "could see the effect of his words by the white gutters made by tears which trickled down the blackened cheeks of the miners, for they came unwashed out of the coal pits to hear him." *(Withrow, 1898, p. 122)* At this time, John Wesley could not yet reconcile himself at first to this type of field preaching. He did not understand people coming to God outside of a church. "At Moorsfields and on Kennington Common the clear ringing voice of Whitefield could be heard by vast multitudes who thronged to hear the new prophet. 'Scores of carriages, hundreds of horsemen, and thirty or forty thousand on foot,' says Dr. Stevens, 'thronged around him. Their singing could be heard two miles off, and his own voice a mile.'" *(Withrow, 1898, p. 122)* Whitefield came to America again in 1739. Over 20,000 people gathered in Boston Common to hear him. In seventy five days he preached 175 sermons. *(Withrow, 1898, p. 123)*

In the midst of this success were troubles. Whitefield and the Wesley brothers had a falling out because Whitefield adopted the doctrine of Election, but he and the Wesley brothers soon reconciled. Whitefield believed in the doctrine of Election because he could not conceive God saving such a wicked person as himself otherwise. He was also persecuted for his preaching. He had stones, dirt, eggs and dead cats thrown at him as he preached in some places. But he continued to preach and some of the persecutors became converts, sometimes up to 300 at a time. In Dublin, Ireland he was viciously attacked by Catholic mobs and injured by rocks. In Edinburgh, Scotland, he preached for 4 weeks straight to 10,000 people per day. He did this despite the fact that he was in poor health much of the time. *(Withrow, 1898, pp. 124-127)*

Whitefield crossed over to Ireland 42 times and to America 13. *(Withrow, 1898, p. 127)*

> "One marked characteristic of Whitefield was his tenderness, his sympathy for sinners, his burning love for souls. He that would move others must himself be moved. Hence multitudes were melted into tears, because tears were in the preacher's words, his voice, and often on his cheeks. 'You blame me for weeping, but how can I help it when you will not weep for yourselves, although your immortal souls are upon the verge of destruction?'" *(Withrow, 1898, p. 131)*

He was tireless in his effort to spread the Gospel and "used to pray that he might die in the pulpit or just after leaving it. His prayer was almost literally granted him." He died on July 29, 1770, shortly after preaching his last sermon. *(Withrow, 1898, p. 131)*

**Selina, Countess of Huntingdon (1707 — 1791):**
Unlike many of the evangelists of more humble backgrounds, Lady Huntingdon was the daughter of the Earl of Ferrers, and connected to the royal family of England.

"In her early life she was married to Theophilus Hastings, Earl of Huntingdon. Lady Elizabeth and Lady Margarot Hastings, her sisters-in-law, had become interested in the Oxford Methodists. Through their influence and through severe personal and family affliction, the Countess was led to a religious life and a strong sympathy with the methods and principles of the evangelists, especially of Whitefield. Her husband sent for Bishop Benson to restore her to a 'saner mind,' but the learned prelate failed in the attempt." *(Withrow, 1898, p. 138)*

Despite her high standing, Lady Huntingdon was not ashamed of the Methodists. When George Whitefield and John and Charles Wesley had their falling out, it was Lady Huntingdon who mediated between them and succeeded in bringing about reconciliation. In 1744 she hosted the Wesleys' first conference. *(Withrow, 1898, pp. 138-139)*

In 1748 Lady Huntingdon became a widow, and devoted her life to the promotion of God's Kingdom. She brought Whitefield in to preach to the nobility of England, and was responsible for many ladies of the nobility becoming followers of Christ. She also came up with a plan to evangelize England. "She divided all England into six districts, to be systematically visited by traveling 'canvassers,' as she called them, who were zealously to preach the Gospel in every village, town and hamlet in the country." She also toured England with other noble ladies accompanied by evangelists and preached to many. When the churches were closed to them, they preached in the fields and the countryside. *(Withrow, 1898, pp. 139-142)*

Following George Whitefield's death, she helped the orphanage in Georgia which he had started. She also sent a principal and a pastor to the orphanage, as well as sending missionaries to work with the blacks and colonists in America. Unfortunately, many of these missionaries had to return to England during the American Revolution. *(Withrow, 1898, pp. 146-147)*

"After her death [in 1791] she left twenty thousand dollars to the poor. The residue of her large fortune was left for the endowment of the sixty-four chapels which had been erected, chiefly through her efforts, in different parts of the kingdom." As a result of her funding these chapels, over 1,000,000 people in Wales came to know Christ. *(Withrow, 1898, pp. 148-149)*

### *Barbara Heck (1734 — 1804):*

Barbara and her husband, Paul Heck, were members of a German community who, through the preaching of John Wesley, became converts to Methodism. They immigrated to New York from Ireland about 1760, and settled in New York, where other Methodists from Ireland arrived about the same time. They had no pastor and, as a result, grew careless in their religion. In 1765, they were joined by Philip Embury, who had been a local preacher in Ireland, and another group of immigrants from Ireland which included her brother Paul Ruckle. Soon after their arrival, Mrs. Heck entered a room in which Philip Embury was present, and found them gambling at cards. She seized the cards and threw them into the fire, told off the players in no uncertain terms, and then went to Embury and demanded that he should preach to them, or God would require their blood at his hands. As a result of her pleading, meetings were shortly afterward begun. The first group included the Hecks and their slave, Betty. Eventually the revival included a large number, mostly Irish immigrants and a number of African Americans. Barbara Heck designed the simple chapel at John Street which represented the group's first permanent location.

During the Revolutionary War, the Hecks, who were loyalists to the British cause, moved to Salem, New York, in order to be among other like-minded people. There they founded the first Methodist society in that district. Paul joined the British army of John Burgoyne, and, while at home on a furlough at the time of the surrender at Saratoga, he was arrested by patriot soldiers. He escaped at night while they slept, and made his way through the woods into Canada, where he was joined by his wife. They settled in Augusta, and with others from New York formed the earliest Methodist society in Canada. *(Heck, Barbara, 2010)*

### *Philip Embury (1729 — 1775):*
"Barbara Heck's eyes blazed as she stood in Philip Embury's living room. 'Philip, you must preach to us, or we shall all go to Hell together and God will require our blood at your hands!'"

This wasn't the first time that Barbara had confronted Philip about this issue. In fact, she'd become an absolute nag on the subject. But Philip could not remember ever seeing her so upset before.

In the old world, Philip had been a Methodist preacher, and he was the first Methodist preacher to settle in Britain's

American colonies. But in America he was too busy trying to make a living to preach. Meanwhile, the Methodists had grown spiritually lukewarm.

Barbara saw the danger. But Philip wasn't so sure. "I cannot preach, for I have neither a house nor congregation." Barbara responded, "Preach in your own house first, and to our own company."

Philip agreed and preached his first sermon to five people in his own rented house. This is believed to be the first Methodist sermon preached in America. After this, Embury held services every Thursday evening and twice on Sunday.

The five people grew to a much larger congregation, and the small congregation had to rent a large room. Stories about the Methodists helped the little church grow, because some of the people who came to check them out were impressed and joined. A Methodist British military man who had been converted in Bristol, England under John Wesley's preaching, also joined Philip. This was Captain Webb, who was a bold evangelist. He began to speak to the neighbors and in the soldiers' barracks and rum shops near where the Methodists rented their hall.

The "little Methodist society began to grow. Eventually it built a church. One of the members wrote a letter to John Wesley, describing the situation and asking for legal advice on how to deed the land. Noting that Embury and Webb lacked training, he added, 'We want an able and experienced preacher; one who has both gifts and grace necessary for the work.' This prompted Wesley to send his first Methodist missionaries to America." *(Graves, 2007)*

### Captain Thomas Webb (1724 — 1796):

Webb was a British army officer in America. He was wounded at Louisburg, Canada, where he lost an eye, and at Quebec, where he was wounded in the arm. After returning to England in 1764, he attended a Methodist meeting and listened to the preaching of John Wesley. He struggled greatly with the concept of sin for a year, but finally reached an assurance of salvation in 1765. Wesley licensed Captain Webb to preach, which he did for the remainder of his life.

Webb was ordered back to the United States, and was stationed in Albany, New York, as barrack master. While there he conducted religious services in his house. When Barbara Heck started the Methodist society in New York City, Captain Webb went there, preaching alternately with Philip Embury. He always wore his regimental British army uniform, complete with his sword either laying on the pulpit, or in a scabbard by his side. This caused quite a stir among the parishioners.

After retiring from the army, Webb began to travel as a missionary throughout New England. He was responsible for starting the first Methodist society in Philadelphia in 1767. The congregation numbered 100 people. In that year he also started Methodist societies in Delaware, and later in Baltimore, Maryland.

In 1772, he went to England, preached in Dublin, London, and other places, making appeals for missionaries to come to America. Captain Webb returned to America in 1774, but was compelled to return to England at the outbreak of the American Revolution. His interest was in the souls of Americans, but, being a patriot, did not agree with the American Revolution. Returning to England, he spent the remainder of his life ministering in the town of Bristol and the surrounding neighborhood. Captain Webb visited Winchester during the war with France, where he preached to the French prisoners in their own language, and addressed large congregations of soldiers and sailors at Portsmouth. He died in 1796 at the age of 72.

> "A high Methodist authority, who knew the captain well, says, 'They saw the warrior in his face, and heard the missionary in his voice. Under his holy eloquence they trembled, they wept, and fell down under his mighty word.'
>
> The native talent of Webb was sustained by considerable intelligence. He had seen much of human life, and had some knowledge of books. He read the Scriptures in the Greek language, and his Greek Testament is still a precious relic in America.
>
> One of Wesley's veterans, who was intimate with the captain, and who read the funeral service over his coffin, says, 'Great multitudes crowded to hear him, and a vast number in different places owned him for their spiritual father. His ministry was plain, but remarkably powerful; he was truly a Boanerges, and often made the stouthearted tremble.'" *(Maxey, 1998)*

### *Dr. Thomas Coke (1747 — 1814):*

Gerald H. Anderson, quoted by The Boston University Theology School website, says this about Thomas Coke:

> "Coke was born in Brecon, Wales, of well-to-do parents. Educated at Jesus College, Oxford University, with a B.A., M.A., and a doctorate in civil law, he worked first as a burgess and bailiff in Brecon, and then as an ordained Anglican curate in South Petherton. Dismissed in 1777 for his Wesleyan leanings, Coke joined John

Wesley, who found in him a valued legal mind, a gifted evangelical preacher, a skilled administrator, and in later years, his most trusted companion. After serving as superintendent of Methodism's London circuit (1780) and first chairman of the Irish Conference (1782), Coke was ordained and appointed by Wesley in 1784 as superintendent for the work in the newly independent United States. Coke convened the organizing conference for American Methodism at Baltimore, Maryland, in 1784 and, with authorization from Wesley, ordained Francis Asbury and consecrated him joint superintendent. Through nine subsequent visits to the growing church in the United States, Coke symbolized the unity of Methodists on both sides of the Atlantic. They threatened slaveholders with excommunication, and presented an antislavery petition to President George Washington at Mount Vernon in 1785.

Coke was rightly called Father of the Methodist Missions . . . [T]he British West Indies and other British colonies became his dominant passion for the remainder of his life. At the last conference attended by John Wesley at Bristol in 1790, Coke was named to head the first Methodist missionary committee. 'I beg from door to door,' he told his friends without embarrassment, and he donated his family's wealth to the missionary effort. Beginning in 1792, he led in sending pioneer missionaries to most islands in the West Indies, as well as to new missions in Sierra Leone, Nova Scotia, Ireland, and France. During the Napoleonic Wars he organized work among the 70,000 French prisoners of war held in England. He died in 1814 on board a ship en route to India, leading a missionary band of preachers for India and South Africa. Wesleyan Methodist missions advanced spectacularly following Coke's death, building on the visionary foundations he had laid." *(Anderson, 1998)*

***Francis Asbury (1745 — 1816):***
Christianity Today's Denominational Founders web page says this about Francis Asbury:

"Some today might call him a workaholic . . . [D]uring his 45-year ministry in America, (Asbury) traveled on horseback or in carriage an estimated 300,000 miles, delivering some 16,500 sermons. He was so well-known in America that letters addressed to 'Bishop Asbury, United States of America' were delivered to him. He put American Methodism on the denominational map.

Asbury was born into a working-class Anglican family; he dropped out of school before he was 12 to work as a blacksmith's apprentice. By the time he was 14, he had been 'awakened' in the Christian faith.

He and his mother attended Methodist meetings, where soon he began to preach; he was appointed a full-time Methodist preacher by the time he was 21. In 1771, at a gathering of Methodist ministers, John Wesley asked, 'Our brethren in America call aloud for help. Who are willing to go over and help them?' Asbury volunteered.

When in October 1771, Asbury landed in Philadelphia, there were only 600 Methodists in America. Within days, he hit the road preaching but pushed himself so hard that he fell ill that winter.

This was the beginning of a pattern: over the next 45 years, he suffered from colds, coughs, fevers, severe headaches, ulcers, and eventually chronic rheumatism, which forced him off his horse and into a carriage. Yet he continued to preach.

During the Revolutionary War, Asbury remained politically neutral. To avoid signing an oath disclaiming his allegiance to England and to dodge the American draft, he went into hiding for several months. 'I am considered by some as an enemy,' he wrote, 'liable to be seized by violence and abused.' By war's end, he had retained his credibility with the victorious Americans and was able to continue his ministry among them.

After the war, John Wesley ordained Englishman Thomas Coke as Wesley's American superintendent. Coke, in turn, ordained Asbury at the famous 'Christmas Conference' of 1784, which gave birth to the American Methodist Episcopal Church. On Christmas Day, Asbury was ordained a deacon, the following day, an elder, and on December 27, a superintendent (against Wesley's advice, Asbury later used the term 'bishop'). As Coke put it, 'We were in great haste and did much business in a little time.' Within six months, Coke returned to England, and thereafter, Asbury held the reins of American Methodism.

Organization was Asbury's gift. He created 'districts' of churches, each of which would be served by circuit riders—preachers who traveled from church to church to preach and minister, especially in rural areas. In the late 1700s, 95 percent of Americans lived in places with fewer than 2,500 inhabitants, and thus most did not have access to church or clergy.

This is one reason Asbury pushed for missionary expansion into the Tennessee and Kentucky frontier— even though his and other preachers' lives were constantly threatened by illness and Indian attacks. According to biographer Ezra Tipple, Asbury's preaching was more zeal than art, and highly effective. Tipple wrote there were occasions when 'under the rush of his utterance, people sprang to their feet as if summoned to the judgment bar of God.'" *(Tipple, 2008)*

### *Gideon Ouseley (1762 — 1839):*
Wesley Weir, writing for the Irish Wesley Genealogy web page, says this about Gideon Ouseley:

> "One of the best known Irish evangelists in the years after John Wesley's death was Gideon Ouseley who preached, often from horseback, at the fairs and markets, both in English and in his native tongue. He was one of a small band of such men who were often called 'Calvary' preachers (an adaption of cavalry) or 'black caps.'
>
> Gideon was born in Galway, to John Ouseley of Dunmore and Anne Surridge of Fairy Hill in the same County. Ouseley's own brother told him off 'for running up and down the country on one wild-goose chase after another, instead of staying at home like a sensible man.' The more sophisticated Methodist congregations disliked him because they didn't want to be constantly reminded of Hell. When he visited Dublin in 1820 he commented to Matthew Tobias in a letter that they 'dreaded the very sight of him.'
>
> A modern historian of Irish Methodism, David Hempton, has concluded that 'for the first quarter of

a century of itinerant labors he ... had been disliked by most of the Catholic clergy, the vast majority of Episcopalian and Presbyterian clergy, and by a powerful group of preachers within his own Connexion [sic]. He had been an embarrassment to most Protestant landlords and posed difficult problems for the civil magistrates.'

Popular with the poor and needy he was shunned by those in authority." *(Weir, 2013)*

### Egerton Ryerson (1803 — 1882):

Claude Doucet, writing for the web page of the Ryerson Library, submitted this biographical sketch of Egerton Ryerson:

"Adolphus Egerton Ryerson was born on March 24, 1803 into a prominent loyalist family in Charlottesville, Norfolk County, in what is now southwestern Ontario. His father, Joseph Ryerson, served on the British side in the American Revolutionary War and also participated, along with his three eldest sons, in the War of 1812. Egerton's youth prevented him from following in their footsteps and he concentrated instead on his studies — he was an avid reader of the classics — and on a deeply religious training fostered by his father's Anglican conservatism and his mother's Methodist radicalism. Forced to choose between the two, he converted to Methodism (much to his father's chagrin) and left the family homestead at the age of 18.

Ryerson started out as a saddle-bag preacher and itinerant minister who rode daily, on horse-back, throughout the Church's Niagara circuit, delivering countless sermons and even living and working with the Ojibway Indians of the Credit River settlement as a missionary. In 1829, as an increasingly vocal proponent of the rights of Methodists and other non-conformist religious groups, he helped found the influential newspaper, the *Christian Guardian*, and served as its intermittent editor for eleven years.

Ryerson's growing prominence in the Methodist community led to his appointment as chief negotiator for his Church in Upper Canada and to his securing a Royal Charter and funding for the establishment of the Upper Canada Academy in Cobourg, an alternative to the Anglican-supported Upper Canada College. The Academy became a University in 1841, with Egerton Ryerson as its principal, and was renamed Victoria College, the forerunner of its current namesake at the University of Toronto. Ryerson also founded the Methodist Book Concern, which later became the Ryerson Press. In honor of his achievements on behalf of the Methodist Church, Egerton Ryerson received a Doctor of Divinity degree from the Wesleyan University in Connecticut and served as President of the Church in Canada from 1874 to 1878.

As politics and religion were inextricably linked in the 19th Century, it is not surprising that Egerton Ryerson played an equally significant and active role on the Canadian political scene, especially with regard to the Clergy Reserves, which had been set aside by the Constitutional Act of 1791 and were then in the exclusive and powerful hands of the Church of England. Ryerson fought for the secularization of the Reserves and for other reforms, alongside such figures as William Lyon Mackenzie. He opposed Mackenzie's radical philosophy and violent methods, however, and emerged as a lifelong moderate and non-partisan voice in the struggle for equality of opportunity within the confines of the law.

A critical issue in the call to secularize the Reserves was the need to reform education and make good schooling accessible to all and not just the privileged few. Having gained a reputation as a man of proven political wisdom and administrative skill, Egerton Ryerson was asked by Governor-General Sir Charles Metcalfe to become Chief Superintendent of Education for Upper Canada in 1844. It is in this realm that Ryerson made his greatest impact and contribution.

Perhaps Egerton Ryerson's most visible achievement was the erection of the Normal School at St. James Square in Toronto in 1852, with its attendant model schools for the in-class training of teachers. In addition to the Normal and Model schools, the buildings housed the Department of Education and served to introduce the citizens of Ontario to a host of artistic, cultural and scientific activities which laid the foundation for publicly-supported museums, art galleries and other institutions in this country." *(Doucet, 2002)*

## *Martin Wells Knapp (1853-1901)*
## *and Seth Cook Rees (1854-1933)*

Martin and Seth were dynamic evangelism pioneers. Knapp in particular was tireless, highly innovative, and effective in his evangelism efforts. Both men had a passion for winning people to Christ, and their emphasis was both international and local. They were often quoted as saying, "Holiness that is not missionary is bogus." *(Drury, 2012, p. 105)* Martin Knapp quickly began an dozen ministries that were a separate from, but complementary to, the Pilgrim Holiness denomination.

Seth Cook Rees joined with Martin Knapp's evangelistic ventures. In 1896 he contacted Knapp for the first time, in Cincinnati. The two men were immediately attracted to one another and cooperated closely from this point in their common task. The association of the two was limited to the five-year period of 1896-1911, being cut short by Knapp's early death, but it was very important to the future Pilgrim Holiness Church." *(Wilson E. L., 2015)*

### Charles Cowman (1868 — 1924):
Charles was a Western Union executive. After coming to Christ at age 31, he led 75 of his fellow workers to Christ in the first six months after becoming a Christian. Charles and his wife, Leittie, later founded the Oriental Mission Society and themselves became missionaries to Japan in 1901. *(Drury, 2012, p. 108)*

## Other Early Evangelism Pioneers: 19th Century
### James Hudson Taylor (1832 — 1905):
This biographical sketch for James Hudson Taylor is presented in the Boston University School of Theology web page:

> "Born at Barnsley, Yorkshire, England, Hudson Taylor sensed by the time he was 17 that God was calling him to China. He prepared himself by reading books on China, analyzing the *Chinese Gospel of Luke*, and studying medicine. Four years of his first term of service (1853-1860) in southeast China was under a Chinese evangelization society, founded under

the inspiration of Karl Gützlaff. In 1858 in Ningpo (Ningbo) he married Maria Dyer, who was a faithful helpmate until her death in 1870.

Although forced to return to England in 1860 because of poor health, Taylor had a continuing concern for the millions of Chinese living in provinces where no missionary had ever gone. In 1865 he summed up his growing vision in *China's Spiritual Need and Claims*. The same year, with great faith but limited financial resources, he founded the China Inland Mission. Its goal was to present the gospel to all the provinces of China. Beginning in 1866 with a group of twenty-two missionaries, including the Taylors, the mission grew rapidly in numbers and outreach. By the time of Taylor's death in 1905, the CIM was an international body with 825 missionaries living in all eighteen provinces of China, more than 300 stations of work, more than 500 local Chinese helpers, and 25,000 Christian converts. Taylor stamped his own philosophy of life and work on the CIM: sole dependence on God financially, with no guaranteed salary; close identification with the Chinese in their way of life; administration based in China itself rather than in Great Britain; an evangelical, nondenominational faith; and an emphasis upon diffusing the gospel as widely as possible through all of China. The last led him to encourage single women to live in the interior of China, a step widely criticized by other mission societies.

With heavy administrative responsibilities, Taylor spent as much time out of China as in, traveling to many countries to make China's needs known and to recruit new missionaries. Although often absent from China, Taylor kept in close touch with his many missionaries, and where possible, continued to engage in missionary activity. He played a prominent part at the General Missionary Conferences in Shanghai in 1877 and 1890. He retired from administration 1901, died in Changsha, Hunan, in 1905, and was buried in Chen-chiang (Zhenjiang), Kiangsu (Jiangsu)." *(Covell, Missionary Biography: J. Hudson Taylor, 2008)*

### *Charles Haddon Spurgeon (1832 — 1892):*

The Spurgeon Archive contains this brief biography of Charles Spurgeon:

> "Spurgeon, Victorian England's best-known Baptist minister, was born on June 19, 1834 in Kelvedon, Essex and spent his childhood and early teenage years in Stambourne, Colchester, and Newmarket. In 1856 he married Susannah Thompson; their only children, twin sons Thomas and Charles, were born on September 20, 1857.
>
> Spurgeon had no formal education beyond Newmarket Academy, which he attended from August 1849 to June 1850, but he was very well-read in Puritan theology, natural history, and Latin and Victorian literature. His lack of a college degree was no hindrance to his remarkable preaching career, which began in 1850, when he was only fifteen years old. A few months after his conversion to Christianity, he began preaching at Teversham. The next year, he accepted his first pastorate, at the Baptist Chapel in Waterbeach. The church quickly grew from fewer

than a dozen congregants to more than four hundred, and Spurgeon's reputation as a preacher caught the attention of New Park Street, London's largest Baptist church. He was invited to preach there in December 1853 and, following a brief probationary period, he agreed to move to London and become the church's new pastor.

Spurgeon's New Park Street congregation grew rapidly as well, soon becoming too large for the 1200-seat auditorium. On August 30, 1854, the membership agreed to enlarge the chapel; during the remodeling, services were held at the 5,000-seat Exeter Hall, a public auditorium in Strand Street. The renovations to New Park Street were complete in May 1855, but the chapel was still too small, and in June a committee was formed to oversee the construction of the church's new home, the 5,000-seat Metropolitan Tabernacle. The congregation moved once again, meeting in Exeter Hall and the 8,000-seat Surrey Gardens Music Hall until the Tabernacle was dedicated on March 18, 1861.

Spurgeon began publishing shortly after he started preaching. In January 1855, Passmore and Alabaster inaugurated the "Penny Pulpit," publishing one sermon every week; the series continued until 1917, a quarter-century after Spurgeon's death.

Spurgeon's preaching was both enormously popular and highly controversial. Some regarded him as the greatest orator since Whitefield; others criticized him as theatrical, awkward, and even sacrilegious. Two of his most controversial works were his "Baptismal Regeneration" sermon and his 'Down Grade' articles. On June 5, 1864, he preached a sermon entitled 'Baptismal Regeneration,' objecting to Anglican teachings on the sacramental power of infant baptism. Over 350,000 copies were sold, and the furor it provoked led to Spurgeon's withdrawal from the Evangelical Alliance, an ecumenical association of Dissenters and Evangelical Anglicans.

The 'Down Grade' controversy began in 1887, when Spurgeon published a series of articles declaring that evolutionary thinking and liberal theology threatened to 'Down Grade' the church. In this case, he was concerned not with Anglican teaching, but with what he believed to be doctrinal error, particularly Unitarian ideas, within the Baptist Union.

Illness forced Spurgeon to keep a low profile during the last few years of his life. He preached his final sermon at the Metropolitan Tabernacle on June 7, 1891. He died in France on January 31, 1892; on February 9, over 60,000 people filed past his casket in the Tabernacle. He was buried at Norwood Cemetery on February 11." *(Spurgeon Archive, n.d.)*

### *Charles Grandison Finney (1792 — 1875):*
The University of Virginia published this biography of Charles Finney:

"Finney's life began in 1792 in the town of Warren, Connecticut. When he was two years old, Finney's parents, like many New Englanders of their day, heeded the call of the frontier and moved to Oneida County in the wilderness of western New York. Although the community had a common school which Finney attended, he and his neighbors had little access to religious services or books. According to his memoirs, written while he was president of Oberlin College, Finney's domestic life did no more to promote religious feeling:

'My parents were neither of them professors of religion, and, I believe, among our neighbors there were very few religious people. I seldom heard a sermon, unless it was an occasional one from some travelling minister, or some miserable holding forth of an ignorant preacher who would sometimes be found in that country. I recollect very well that the ignorance of the preachers that I heard was such that the people would return from meeting and spend a considerable time in irrepressible laughter at the strange mistakes which had been made and the absurdities which had been advanced.'

All that changed, however, in the autumn of 1808. At age twenty-nine, [Finney], a student of the law in Adams, New York, was saved. One Wednesday morning Charles Finney woke up a questioning and sometimes scornful observer of the religious life around him. The following day, when asked by a client if he were ready to try the case scheduled for that day, Finney was able to reply, 'I have a retainer from the Lord Jesus Christ, to plead his cause. I cannot plead yours.'

The ministry which began that day would change the face of American evangelism. Before and after his conversion, Finney rejected the Calvinist doctrine of passive salvation available only to the elect. He believed that God offered Himself to everyone and, most importantly, that one could be saved only through an active acceptance of God's invitation to grace. The sinner chooses to sin just as the penitent chooses to repent.

To reach as many souls as possible, Finney employed what came to be called 'new measures,' although many had been used by earlier preachers. These new measures triggered alarm among conservative clergy. Opponents such as Asahel Nettleton were able to list as many as twenty-nine objectionable practices, but the most controversial were: public praying of women in mixed-sex audiences, daily services over a series of days, use of colloquial language by the preacher, the 'anxious bench,' praying for people by name, and immediate church membership for converts.

Ordained a Presbyterian minister in 1824, Finney was soon at odds with conservative clergy. The new methods used by Finney and his followers caused enough alarm among their more orthodox colleagues to be the subject of a convention held at New Lebanon, NY in July, 1827. Motions were made to restrict the New School revivalists, but no definitive anti-new measures resolution was effected. The victory for Finney and his fellows was in emerging relatively unscathed from a confrontation with powerful clergymen like Lyman Beecher.

In the years following New Lebanon, Finney's ministry moved from small town to big city; he went on to preach in Philadelphia, Boston, and New York. In 1835 he began work in Oberlin College and Theological Seminary. He was President of Oberlin College from 1851 to 1866 and although he retired in 1872, Finney kept up his involvement with Oberlins students until his death in August of 1875." *(Finney, n.d.)*

***Dwight L. Moody (1837-1899):***
The official web page for the Moody Bible Institute presents this biographical information about D. L. Moody:

> "Moody (February 5, 1837-December 22, 1899) was born the sixth child of Edwin and Betsy Holton Moody in Northfield, Mass. on February 5, 1837. Dwight's formal education ended in the fifth grade, and he rapidly tired of life on the farm. He left home at age 17, seeking employment in Boston. Failing to secure a desirable position, he asked his uncle, Samuel Holton, for a job. Reluctantly, Uncle Samuel hired him to work in the retail shoe store he owned. However, to keep young Moody out of mischief, employment was conditional upon his attendance at the Mt. Vernon Congregational Church. At Mt. Vernon Moody became part of the Sunday school class taught by Edward Kimball. On April 21, 1855, Kimball visited the Holton Shoe Store, found Moody in a stockroom, and there spoke to him of the love of Christ. Shortly thereafter, Moody accepted that love and devoted his life to serving God. The following year brought Moody to Chicago with dreams of making his fortune in the shoe business. As success in selling shoes came, so did an interest in providing a Sunday school class for Chicago's children and the local Young Men's Christian Association (YMCA)
> 
> Moody's Mission Sunday School flourished. What set this school apart was Moody's desire to reach the 'lost' youth of the city, the children with little to no education, less than ideal family situations, and poor economic circumstances. Soon the Sunday school

outgrew the converted saloon used as a meeting hall. As the classes grew, associates encouraged Moody to begin his own church. Eventually, on Feb. 28, 1864, the Illinois Street Church (now The Moody Church) opened in its own building with Moody as pastor.

In June 1872, Moody made his first trip to the United Kingdom, during which a few close contacts urged him to come back in a year. In June 1873, Moody, with his wife Emma, their children, good friend and musician Ira Sankey and his wife all traveled from New York to Liverpool, England. Moody and Sankey traveled throughout the U.K. and Ireland holding meetings, helping to fuel the revival that was slowly sweeping the region. Moody's visit made a lasting impression, inspiring lay people across the region to begin children's ministries and ministry training schools for women.

Moody was revolutionary in his evangelistic approach. Despite conflicting counsel from friends and trusted contacts, he and Sankey traveled to Ireland during a time when Catholics and Protestants were constantly at odds with each other. Moody was different: he did not care what denomination a person claimed, but just wanted the message of Christ to be heard. As a result, the revival swept into Ireland, and he won praises of both Catholics and Protestants.

Moody was on the cutting edge of ministry, and in 1879, Moody opened the Northfield Seminary for Young Women to provide young women the opportunity to gain an education. Not long after, Moody created the Mount Hermon School for Boys with the same goal as the girls' school — to educate the poor and minorities. Moody had an amazing ability to bridge the gap between denominations, which was apparent in the diverse religious backgrounds of the school's students.

Moody continued to evangelize throughout America, often preaching in major cities and at various universities. His heart was for his schools, and he spent much of his time in Northfield. Moody was a visionary who always seemed a step ahead of the status quo. From training women, to reaching out to lost children, to bridging the gap between denominations, he was unlike any other.

Moody was a man of great discernment. He had an innate ability to find capable, godly people to put into positions of leadership and bring his ideas to fruition. This enabled him to continue his evangelistic outreach while his ministries flourished. Throughout his life, Moody always found time to be with his family, making every effort to show his love and care for them." *(D. L. Moody's Story, n.d.)*

CHAPTER 5

# Evangelism Giants: 20th and 21st Century

### R. A. Torrey (1856-1928):

The Christian Biography Resources website contains this short biography of R. A. Torrey

> "R. A. Torrey was American evangelist, pastor, educator, and writer. He was called by D. L. Moody to head Bible Institute in Chicago (now Moody Bible Institute). He was also the Dean of Bible Institute of Los Angeles. Torrey's pastorates included Chicago Avenue Church (now Moody Memorial) and Church of the Open Door, Los Angeles. He held worldwide evangelistic meetings with Charlie Alexander and founded Montrose Bible Conference, Pennsylvania. Torrey wrote more than forty books." *(Christian Biography Resources: R. A. Torrey, 2015)*

### Gypsy Smith (1860-1947):

The biblebelievers.com website contains this biographical sketch of Gypsy Smith.

> "Gypsy Smith was born in a tent, raised on a Gypsy camp, never attended a school , yet he influenced

the lives of millions of people for God through his powerful preaching. He was converted in 1876 and, the next year, was invited by General William Booth to join him in evangelistic work. He served as an officer with the Salvation Army until 1882. He then began ministering as an itinerant evangelist working with a variety of organizations all over the world, but particularly in Britain and America." *(Smith, n.d.)*

### Billy Sunday (1862-1935):

On the Wheaton College Institute for the Study of American Evangelicals is recorded this biography of Billy Sunday:

"Born near Ames, Iowa the son of a tenant farmer and wife, he spent most of his teen years in an orphanage and working as a hired farm laborer. A superb baseball player with lightning speed he was signed to a contract with the Chicago White Stockings (today's Chicago Cubs) in 1883 and spent seven years in the National League setting a record for most stolen bases that was later broken by Ty Cobb.

In 1886, after a night's carousing in Chicago, Sunday was converted at the city's Pacific Garden Mission. Becoming active with the YMCA and at a local Presbyterian Church, Sunday married in 1888 and retired from baseball in 1890 in favor of preaching the Gospel. After a full-time stint with the YMCA, Sunday served three years under the tutelage of famed evangelist J. Wilbur Chapman before launching his own career in 1896.

Over the next four decades Sunday would become the most prolific American evangelist since D.L.

Moody, conducting over 250 campaigns throughout the nation. Railing against sin, alcohol, and vice, his theatrical style and verbal broadsides garnered immense publicity and newspaper coverage wherever he preached. Often Sunday's campaigns lasted for several weeks at a time in such cities as New York, Chicago and Philadelphia. Committees of local citizens and businessmen seeking to fight crime, promote clean, sober living and the development of responsible, hard-working employees frequently issued the invitation and footed the bill to get Sunday to come to town.

In the process, Sunday gained a comfortable lifestyle, a great deal of personal wealth, and no shortage of criticism, even though he gave most of his fortune away. Sunday's popularity waned as the 1920s progressed and his pro-Temperance sentiments and old-fashioned diatribes against sin fell increasingly out of style. Nonetheless, it is estimated that perhaps as many as 100 million people heard Sunday preach and that over one million people walked down the 'Sawdust Trail' to shake his hand and accept Christ as their savior." *(Billy Sunday, n.d.)*

### *Mordecai Ham (1877-1961):*

This biographical information of Mordecai Ham was located on Ranker.com's web page:

"Mordecai Fowler Ham, Jr., was an American Independent Baptist evangelist and temperance movement leader. He entered the ministry in 1901 and in 1936 began a radio broadcast reaching into seven southern states. Early in his ministry, he was ordained at Burton Memorial Baptist Church in Bowling Green, Kentucky. 'From the time I was eight years old, I never thought of myself as anything but a Christian. At nine, I had definite convictions that the Lord wanted me to preach . . . .' Ham studied at Ogden College in Bowling Green and relocated to Chicago, Illinois, where he engaged in business from 1896-1900. There, he married the former Bessie Simmons in July 1900. In December 1900, he closed the business to devote full-time to the ministry.

One target of Ham's sermons was alcohol abuse, particularly before the adoption of the Eighteenth Amendment to the United States Constitution. He believed that problems involving liquor could best be resolved by conversion to Christianity and the placement of new believers in churches which stress abstinence of alcoholic beverages." *(Mordecai Ham, n.d.)* It was at a revival meeting being held by Mordecai Ham that Billy Graham at age 16 came forward and gave his life to Christ.

### Bob Jones Sr. (1883-1968):

The Institute for the Study of American Evangelicals, Wheaton College, includes this biography of Bob Jones, Sr.

> "Robert Reynolds 'Bob' Jones, Sr., evangelist and founder of Bob Jones University, was born in rural Dale County in southeastern Alabama. A Methodist, Jones was converted at a revival meeting when he was eleven years old and by the time he was fourteen he had begun preaching. Jones attended Southern

University (today's Birmingham Southern College) for three years but did not finish a degree, opting instead to concentrate on evangelistic work. A militant fundamentalist, Jones conducted a wide-ranging campaign denouncing modernist teachings on the Bible and evolution and the abandonment of traditional Protestant social mores. Viewing the control of education as the key to defending the faith, Jones started Bob Jones College near Panama City, Florida in 1927. The financial burden of the Depression caused Jones to move the school to Cleveland, Tennessee in 1933, and financial considerations likewise played a major role in the school's final move to Greenville, South Carolina in 1947 (where it became Bob Jones University). Jones was an early supporter of the National Association of Evangelicals (NAE) but by the mid-1950s had broken with the movement, largely over its support of Billy Graham (who had left the school after his freshman year), whom Jones and his militant son Bob Jones, Jr. viewed as a compromiser for his inclusion of mainline clergy in his evangelistic crusades.

Increasingly, Bob Jones, Sr. and Jr. and their University were seen as the embodiment of ultra-separatist fundamentalism. Although the school emphasized a film school and prided itself on its Shakespearian productions and art collection, the Jones' insistence on rigid social policies and the maintenance of on-campus segregation (black students were not admitted until 1971 and a ban against interracial dating was in place until 2000) made it a symbol in the popular press and among many evangelicals of the backward-looking mindset of the fundamentalist movement." *(Bob Jones Sr., n.d.)*

### Aimee Semple McPherson (1890 — 1944):

Biography.com included this biographical sketch for McPherson:

> "Aimee Semple McPherson was born October 9, 1890, near Ingersoll, Ontario. Her first official sermon occurred at Mount Forest, Ontario, in 1915. In 1918, she made her headquarters in L.A., where she preached in the Angelus Temple for almost 20 years. In 1923, the temple was dedicated as the Church of the Foursquare Gospel. By 1944, her movement had grown to include some 400 U.S. and Canadian branches." *(Aimee Semple McPherson, n.d.)*

### Hyman Appleman (1902-1983):

Believersweb.com website contains this biography of Hyman Appleman.

> "[There are few whose] ministry has been as effective, far reaching and productive as that of this converted Jew. He actually helped spearhead the modern-day swing to mass evangelism, as his city-wide endeavors in the early forties whipped up enthusiasm for evangelism that was all but forgotten since the era of Billy Sunday, Mordecai Ham and Bob Jones, Sr.
>
> He was born on the banks of the Dnieper River in White Russia of Orthodox Jewish parents. He was reared and trained in the Jewish faith by a strict

grandfather and grandmother. Appelman's family moved to America in 1914. In 1925 Appleman met with Dr. James Davis of the Christian Church in Denver in 1925. Upon hearing Romans 10:9 Appleton asked for it to be explained. Finally, through clenched teeth, he said, 'Lord, I do not know, and I do not understand, but this man says and this Book says that Your Son died for my sins, and that if I ask You to, for His sake, You will forgive my sins. Lord, for Jesus' sake, do forgive my sins.' During his life, Appelman's schedule of meetings left one breathless. It was hard to find a day in 45 years when he was not preaching somewhere. An average Appelman year would see some 7,000 first-time professions of faith. By 1969 he had seen over 345,000 total decisions for Christ, with some 270,000 uniting with churches and over 125,000 rededications by Christians. With the day of city-wide crusades waning, Appelman, in his last years on the earth, became a local church evangelist, but his results in single-church meetings were just as large." *(Hyman Jedidiah Appleman, 2003)*

## *Torrey Johnson (1909-2002):*

Wikipedia records this biographical sketch of Torrey Johnson.

"Torrey Johnson was a Chicago evangelist who is best remembered as the founder of Youth for Christ in 1944. For a time Johnson had his own local radio program called "Songs in the Night" which he later turned over to Billy Graham who was also hired as the first full time evangelist employed by Youth for Christ International." *(Torrey Johnson, 2015)*

## Ford Philpot (1917-1992):

The Asbury University website contains this biography of Ford Philpot.

"Ford Philpot was born June 16, 1917, in Clay County, Kentucky. He dropped out of high school only weeks before graduation and moved to Cincinnati in search of work. While working back in Kentucky at Renfro Valley, he met Virginia Robinson, and they were married in 1940. In 1942 Ford joined the Marines and served three years overseas during World War II. In 1947, as Philpot began to emerge from under alcoholism, he enrolled at Asbury College in Wilmore, Kentucky. At Asbury, Philpot was given the opportunity to preach and found it to be his life calling. After graduating from Asbury in 1950, Philpot went on to seminary at Emory University and was ordained in the Methodist Church.

Philpot was widely known as a revival preacher. In his first 15 years of ministry, he preached over 600 crusades around the world. He also produced a 30-minute radio program with his friend, Herb Bowdoin, called 'The Waves of Truth,' which was broadcast throughout central Kentucky. In 1959, Bowdoin and Philpot began producing the first color religious television broadcast called *The Story*, which debuted on WLEX-18 in Lexington, Kentucky, on March 18th, 1960. It is estimated that the show, which included music, testimony from a special guest, and a message by Philpot, reached five million people each week. The program ran for 30 years with more than 900 segments taped. In 1966 'The Story' became

the first religious television program to air in Japan."
(Kinnell, n.d.)

## Billy Graham (1918 - ):

The Biography.com site gives this sketch of Billy Graham's life:

> "Christian evangelist William Franklin Graham, Jr. was born on November 7, 1918, in Charlotte, North Carolina, to parents William and Morrow Graham. Billy Graham was the first of four children raised on the family's dairy farm in Charlotte. In hindsight there was little indication that Graham would one day preach the Christian gospel to as many as 215 million people in live audiences over 185 countries. Graham has been credited with preaching to more individuals than anyone else in history, not counting the additional millions he has addressed through radio, television and the written word.
> 
> While Graham's parents were strict Calvinists, it would be an unfamiliar traveling evangelist who would set Graham on a profound spiritual path. At the age of 16, Graham attended a series of revival meetings run by evangelist Mordecai Ham. Despite the fact that Graham was a well-behaved adolescent, Ham's sermons on sin spoke to young Graham. After high school Graham moved to Tennessee to enroll in the conservative Christian school, Bob Jones College. However, he felt disconnected from the school's rigid doctrine and soon transferred to the Florida Bible Institute. While in Florida, Graham joined a Southern Baptist Convention church, where he was ordained in 1939.

Graham briefly pastored the First Baptist Church in Western Springs, Illinois, before leaving to join Youth for Christ, an evangelical missionary group which spoke to returning servicemen and young people about God. It did not take long for people to identify with Billy Graham's charismatic and heartfelt gospel sermons. In 1949, a group called "Christ for Greater Los Angeles" invited Graham to preach at their L.A. revival. When radio personality Stuart Hamblen had Graham on his radio show, word of the revival spread. The publicity filled Graham's tents and extended the revival for an additional five weeks. At the urging of newspaper magnate William Randolph Hearst, papers around the nation covered Graham's revival meetings closely... As a consequence, Graham became a Christian superstar.

Once a week he also hosted a program called *The Hour of Decision*, a program ABC initially transmitted to 150 stations before reaching its peak of 1,200 stations across America. Eventually this program was converted into a television show which ran for three years. The success of Graham's radio and television programs speak to his role as a Christian media visionary. Graham used the media as a means for spreading the gospel of Christ, allowing him to access millions of people around the globe.

Graham's detractors have criticized him for being too liberal and refusing to play into partisan politics. Fundamentalists wrote him off when he condemned violence perpetrated by the anti-abortion group 'Operation Rescue.' Theologian Reinhold Niebuhr has called him 'simplistic,' while evangelist

Bob Jones believes Graham has done 'more harm to the cause of Jesus Christ than any other living man.' President Truman even went so far as to call Graham a 'counterfeit.' However, through his long and extraordinary career, Graham has overwhelmingly been regarded in a positive light.

In a video entitled *My Hope America*, he expressed concern for the spiritual health of the nation. 'Our country's in great need of a spiritual awakening,' he said, according to a report in *USA Today*. 'There have been times that I've wept as I've gone from city to city and I've seen how far people have wandered from God.'" *(Billy Graham, n.d.)*

### Oral Roberts (1918-2009):

The CNN website gave this biographical sketch of Oral Roberts in its obituary of him in 2009:

"Granville Oral Roberts was born into poverty in Bebee, Oklahoma, on January 24, 1918, according to a brief biography released by Ethridge. His Christian ministry began with what he described as his own miracle healing of tuberculosis at age 17. Roberts pastored churches in Oklahoma and Georgia and preached at revivals around the country while studying at Oklahoma Baptist University and Phillips University in Oklahoma. In 1947, he founded the Oral Roberts Evangelistic Association in Tulsa, 'and began conducting crusades across America and around the world, attracting crowds of thousands — many who were sick and dying and in search of healing,' his biography said. In 1954, he brought television cameras into services, providing what he liked to call a 'front-row seat to miracles' to viewers, the biography said. He later began a television program, initially called 'Oral Roberts Presents.'

Roberts founded the Abundant Life Prayer Group in 1958 'to address the around-the-clock needs of those suffering and requesting prayer,' according to the biography. Today, prayer partners at Abundant Life continue to receive calls 24 hours a day. The group has received more than 23 million phone calls for prayer, the biography said.

Oral Roberts University was founded in 1963, built on 500 acres in Tulsa and dedicated four years later by Graham, according to the biography. Graduate schools including medicine, nursing, dentistry, law, education and theology were later added. He remained involved in his evangelistic association as much as his health allowed. His son, Richard Roberts, currently serves as president." *(Evangelist Oral Roberts dead at 91, 2009)*

**Grady Wilson (1919-1987):**

The New York Times provided this obituary of Grady Wilson:

> "Grady Wilson was ordained a Baptist minister at the age of 18. For 30 years he traveled with Mr. Graham as an associate evangelist, filling in for Mr. Graham on occasion. A member of the original Billy Graham Team, he became a vice president of the Billy Graham Evangelistic Association when it was founded in 1950."
> *(Obituaries, 1987)*

## Howard O. Jones (1921-2010):

The Billy Graham Evangelistic Association website contains this biographical information of Howard Jones.

"As the first black associate evangelist of the Billy Graham Evangelistic Association (BGEA), Jones traveled the world with Graham and handled much of the groundwork for the evangelist's African crusade in 1960. He was the principal speaker for BGEA's 'Hour of Freedom' radio broadcast for 35 years and became the first African American to be inducted into the National Religious Broadcasters Hall of Fame in 1995.

Attending high school in Oberlin, Jones played saxophone in a jazz band but gave up music for ministry. He graduated from Oberlin High School and Nyack College in New York. He married Wanda K. Young of Oberlin in 1944.

Jones spent eight years as pastor of Bethany Christian Missionary Alliance Church in the Bronx, N.Y., and began preaching on the radio there. Then came six years as pastor of Smoot Memorial Christian Missionary Alliance Church in Cleveland. In 1957, he spent three months in Liberia. He was returning to Cleveland through New York when Graham asked him to help integrate a pending crusade at Madison Square Garden. Jones led big rallies in Harlem and Brooklyn and persuaded many worshipers to join him downtown." *(Chismer, 2010)*

***Leighton Ford (1930- ):***

The following biographical information came from Leighton Ford's website.

> "Leighton's call to the ministry of evangelism began when he was very young. From the outset of his life in ministry he was encouraged and guided by significant mentors. These mentors; Evon Hedley, Billy Graham, and Jack Dain, cared about and had concern for Leighton, not just their own agendas. They cared for him as Paul did Timothy, the protégé of whom Paul wrote that he had 'a genuine interest in your welfare' (Philippians 2: 20,21). Over three decades Leighton has had the privilege of preaching in many countries, to large crowds. At the same time his great joy, along with seeing people come to faith in Christ, was to meet and encourage younger men and women, to be a friend to them, and to see them emerge into their own calling as leaders." *(Leighton Ford Ministries, 2015)*

***Clyde Dupin (1933 - ):***

This biography of Dr. Clyde Dupin was obtained from the Clyde Dupin Ministries website:

> "Dr. Clyde Dupin is one of America's most experienced and successful Crusade Evangelists. He conducted his first city-wide Crusade as a 19-year-old college student. He has traveled more than two million miles in Evangelism and preached face-to-face to over four million people. He has devoted more than 50 years to full-time evangelism and has conducted more than

four hundred Crusades. This interdenominational ministry has taken him to 40 different countries. In a Crusade in Port-au-Prince, Haiti, 45,000 people attended the final Crusade service. He has conducted nine Crusades in Russia where 37,500 people have made decisions for Christ. He is an ordained minister and devotes most of his time to speaking for area-wide interdenominational Crusades throughout America and missionary Crusades abroad.

He was born and reared near Elizabethtown, Kentucky. He became a Christian at the age of nine and began his ministry as a boy preacher. He received his theological training at United Wesleyan College and later attended the University of Evansville in Indiana. He holds a honorary Doctor of Divinity degree from Southern Wesleyan University.

Dr. Dupin is known as a gifted communicator of the Gospel whose message is current and relevant. His message speaks to the unchurched and is easily understood. He is the author of three books. His biography, *The Evangelist,...* is an exciting story of twentieth century evangelism. His weekly newspaper column, *Religious Viewpoint*, is published in newspapers throughout the United States and has a potential one million readers each week.

For ten years he pastored Trinity Wesleyan Church in Evansville, Indiana. Under his leadership the church tripled in both Sunday school and church attendance and became one of the largest churches in the denomination. For ten years he conducted a weekly radio broadcast. He served as President of the Greater Evansville Association of Clergymen and was on the Board of Directors for Tri-State Youth for Christ, Inc.

He was an associate with Bill Glass for six years and served as Vice-president of the Bill Glass Evangelistic Association. Since 1974, he has served as President and Evangelist for the Clyde Dupin Ministries." *(Clyde Dupin, n.d.)*

### Dr. Ralph S. Bell (1934-):

Encyclopedia.com has this information on Dr. Ralph S. Bell.

"Ralph S. Bell is an associate evangelist with the Billy Graham Evangelistic Association. One of three Christian ministers handpicked by Dr. Graham to help lead the Billy Graham crusades, Bell assists in every aspect of the popular mass Christian meetings. He also holds city-wide and single-church crusades of his own and addresses Christian topics on radio and television shows. Since 1965 Bell has been directly involved in every major Billy Graham crusade, and since 1980 he has led more than 30 smaller crusades himself." *(Anne Johnson, 1994)*

### Bill Glass (1935 - ):

The Bill Glass organization provided this biography on their website:

"He made a name for himself as one of the most outstanding football players in the National Football League. He was a consensus All American at Baylor University . Working with his life-long friend, Dr. Bill Bright, he helped establish the Campus Crusade for

Christ chapter on the Baylor Campus. He was a member of the 1964 Cleveland Browns team who beat the Baltimore Colts to win the NFL World Championship two years prior to the first Super Bowl. Four-time All Pro and College and Texas Sports Hall of Fame were some of Bill's athletic credentials. He finally retired in 1969 after 22 years in amateur and professional football without missing a work out or game.

Bill spent the off-season of his Pro Football career attending Southwestern Seminary. As his football career was drawing to a close, Bill delivered his personal testimony of faith on television during several Billy Graham Crusades. Dr. Graham urged Bill to consider taking on a new career as a city-wide evangelist.

In 1969 he founded Bill Glass Ministries, which today is called *Bill Glass Behind the Walls*. After spending all those years playing football in front of thousands, he now shares the Good News with thousands. The highlight of his life has been sharing 'The Healing Power of a Father's Blessing' message in and out of prisons all over the world." *(Bill Glass, n.d.)*

### Luis Palau (1937 - ):

About.com included this biography of Luis Palau:

"Luis Palau is [an] evangelist and founder of the Luis Palau Association. He is best known for his worldwide contemporary evangelistic festivals. Palau is a native of Buenos Aires, Argentina. He began his preaching ministry at age 18 by sharing the gospel on the streets of Buenos Aires. In the 1990s his ministry focus moved toward the United States as well as worldwide and by the end of the 1990s he had developed a unique festival evangelism ministry.

Embracing contemporary life and culture, these festivals combine popular music, action sports, family-friendly entertainment, and most importantly, the message of the gospel of Jesus Christ. More than a billion people worldwide have heard him preach the Good News through festivals, radio, television, and the internet.

Born and raised in a wealthy Argentinian family, Luis Palau became a Christian at an early age. By 10 his father died, and Luis assumed the responsibility of supporting his family. He became successful in the banking business before moving to Portland, Oregon where he attended Multnomah Biblical Seminary.

After attending Multnomah Biblical Seminary, Luis Palau and his wife began traveling as missionaries in Latin America. This led to involvement in evangelistic ministries, developing teams and helping evangelists. During this time he interpreted for Billy Graham, who had a big influence on Palau's ministry. Doors of ministry continued to open through international invitations and by the early 1980s Palau was having a big impact in Western Europe.

In the 1990s his ministry focus moved toward the United States as well as worldwide and by the end of the 1990s, through the encouragement of his sons, he developed a unique festival evangelism ministry. The Luis Palau Association holds 4-6 major events in the United States and overseas each year. The festivals are always free and open to everyone. They include multimedia productions, popular Christian music artists, a massive skate park featuring top Christian athletes of action sports like skate boarding, BMX and motocross. There's something for the whole family.

Taken from his biography, Palau states, 'We emphasize Christ more than Christianity or denominations . . . We focus on what Christians are for, not what we might be against. As an evangelist, my role is to share the Good News of our Savior: we leave the politics to others.' Luis Palau's dream is to see an international revival with millions discovering the Christ of Christianity." *(Luis Palau, n.d.)*

### James Robison (1943 - ):

James Robison's website, lifetoday.com, provides this biographical sketch.

"Since 1962, James Robison has delivered the Gospel to the masses — first, through crusade evangelism and for more than 40 years, via television. God led James into the ministry when he was only 18. James began speaking in churches, and doors quickly opened for him to hold crusades in stadiums and indoor arenas nationwide. More than 20 million people attended those meetings, with more than 2 million decisions for Christ. The ministry James founded — LIFE Outreach International — now focuses on television and mission outreaches, and more people are coming to Christ in a single year than in his first 20 years of ministry.

James Robison's background is hardly typical of a nationally-known inspirational leader. He was born in

1943 in the charity ward of a Houston hospital, the product of a forced sexual encounter. His 41-year-old mother originally sought an abortion, but the doctor would not comply. After putting an ad in the newspaper, his mother gave him up to Rev. and Mrs. H.D. Hale, pastors in the Houston suburb of Pasadena. He would remain with them for a few years, until his mother reclaimed him as a young boy and took him to her home in Austin, where they lived in extreme poverty. James' biological father entered their lives when James was a teenager, and after many volatile years in Austin, James nearly shot his alcoholic, ill-tempered father in self-defense. When James returned to Pasadena to visit his foster parents, that short visit changed everything. Mrs. Hale led the teenage boy to the Lord during a revival service. Fortunately, he was able to live with the Hales for his last two years of high school, where he met Betty Freeman. Betty was born in a working class home in Lufkin, Texas, along with her three siblings. Her parents raised her in a Christian home, and when they relocated to Pasadena, they attended the Baptist church pastored by Rev. Hale."

*(James and Betty Robison, 2015)*

### *Ray Comfort (1949 - )*

The official Living Waters web page included this information regarding Ray Comfort:

> "Ray Comfort is the Founder/President/CEO of Living Waters Publications. After relocating from New Zealand to Southern California in the late 1980s,

Ray introduced a long line of pastors and churches to a biblical teaching which he called Hell's Best Kept Secret. The positive and enthusiastic response that followed took Ray's Living Waters Publications ministry to a whole new level. From humble beginnings, LWP has become an internationally recognized ministry, reaching the lost and equipping Christians with every necessary resource to fulfill the great commission.

Ray Comfort is the co-host (with Kirk Cameron) of the award-winning television program 'The Way of the Master,' which airs in 123 countries around the world. Ray is a best-selling author of more than 70 books. He and his wife, Sue, live in Southern California, where they have three grown children." *(Ray Comfort, n.d.)*

### Franklin Graham (1952 - ):

Samaritan's Purse provides this biographical sketch for Franklin Graham:

> "Franklin Graham has devoted his life to meeting the needs of people around the world and proclaiming the Gospel of Jesus Christ. The elder son of Billy and Ruth Bell Graham, he has served as president and CEO of Samaritan's Purse since 1979 and as president and CEO of the Billy Graham Evangelistic Association since 2001. Under his leadership, Samaritan's Purse has met the needs of poor, sick, and suffering people in more than 100 countries. As an evangelist for the Billy Graham Evangelistic Association, he has led crusades around the world.

[Franklin] was born into a heritage rich in Christian ministry. By the time of Franklin's birth, Billy Graham was already known around the world as a spiritual leader, but he wasn't the only spiritual giant in the family. Franklin's maternal grandfather, Lemuel Nelson Bell, was a medical missionary to China for more than 20 years, a respected moderator of his denomination, the Presbyterian Church in the United States, and a co-founder and executive editor of Christianity Today.

At age 22, after a period of rebellion and traveling the world, Franklin committed his life to Jesus Christ while alone in a hotel room in Jerusalem. Soon after that, Dr. Bob Pierce, founder of Samaritan's Purse (and World Vision), invited Franklin to join him on a six-week mission to Asia. It was during that time that Franklin felt a calling to work with hurting people in areas of the world affected by war, famine, disease, and natural disasters." *(Franklin Graham, n.d.)*

CHAPTER 6

# Categories of Approved Evangelists within the Wesleyan Church

Within the Wesleyan Denomination, there are currently three recognized categories of evangelists. As described by the *Discipline of the Wesleyan Church*, an "evangelist is an ordained minister or commissioned or licensed minister who devotes time to traveling and preaching the gospel without any specific pastoral assignment, who is authorized by the Church to promote revivals and spread the gospel of Jesus Christ abroad in the land." The district conferences within the Church may appoint ministers to be General Evangelists, Associate General Evangelists and Reserve Evangelists.

Before being appointed, "the candidate shall be examined carefully by the district board of ministerial development relative to personal Christian experience, full personal commitment to and support of the Articles of Religion and Covenant Membership Commitments, to the government, institutions and best interests of the Wesleyan Church, gifts and aptitudes for the work of an evangelist, and the intention to devote time to the work of evangelism." *(Discipline of the Wesleyan Church, 2012, pp. 278-286)*

*Associate General Evangelist:*

This is an ordained, commissioned or licensed minister appointed to serve as an evangelist, and who devotes a major portion of their time to evangelism. They serve for a minimum of two years. Following their initial year, they must conduct a minimum of 40 services devoted to evangelism each year.

*General Evangelist:*

This is an ordained minister that is appointed by the district conference. They must first serve two years as an Associate General Evangelist. However, this two year requirement may be waived if the district conference determines that the candidate is uniquely qualified to serve in the capacity of General Evangelist. If the district conference recommends the appointment of this person as a General Evangelist, the recommendation goes to the General Superintendent and the Executive Director of Church Multiplication and Discipleship for approval. Upon this approval, a certificate of appointment is issued. The appointment and certification as a General Evangelist is continued in subsequent years if the General Evangelist reports a minimum of 80 services a year devoted to evangelism. If they do not meet this requirement, they are reclassified as an Associate Evangelist or Reserve Evangelist.

*Reserve Evangelist:*

This is an ordained minister who, because of age or physical disability, is limited in their activity. This designation is given by the district. A Reserve Evangelist is required to hold a satisfactory level of evangelist services per year as decided by the district board of ministerial development.

### Special Worker:

This is a lay person with a sense of God's calling to be a director of music, director of spiritual formation or education, youth director, children's worker, lay evangelist, spouse in ministry, music evangelist, children's director, song evangelist, or other area and who has been authorized to do such a work by their district conference.

Within the Wesleyan denomination, there is currently this breakout of these categories:
- 2 Special Workers
- 10 General Evangelists
- 11 Associate General Evangelists
- 3 Reserve Evangelists

The geographical breakout of these individuals within the Wesleyan Church is as follows:

| District | Number (Breakout by Type) |
|---|---|
| Central Canada | 2 (2 Associate) |
| Illinois | 1 (1 Associate) |
| Indiana | 6 (1 Associate, 3 General, 1 Special, 1 Reserve) |
| Florida | 1 (1 Reserve) |
| Kentucky | 1 (1 Associate) |
| Michigan (West) | 3 (2 General, 1 Associate) |
| Michigan (North) | 1 (1 Special) |
| Mountain | 1 (1 General) |
| North Carolina | 4 (3 Associate, 1 Reserve) |
| Ohio | 1 (1 General) |
| Pennsylvania | 1 (1 Associate) |
| South Carolina | 1 (1 Associate) |
| Shenandoah | 2 (2 General) |
| Tennessee | 1 (1 General) |

CHAPTER 7

# Evangelism Training

What follows are course requirements and resources for evangelism classes, as stated in the various course syllabi provided to us by several Wesleyan Church colleges and universities. The scope and depth of the courses offered is impressive, as is the obvious care for the student's grasping the concept of evangelism as it relates to ministry. What is also noticeable is the hands-on approach to evangelism that several of these courses demand, requiring the student to move beyond mere theory into practice. *Note: This is not to be considered a comprehensive list of all courses offered on evangelism at all Wesleyan colleges, universities and seminaries. There may be additional courses offered of which we were not made aware.*

## Houghton College: Houghton, New York
### HC: Evangelism and Church Health: Equipping for Ministry

*Course Description*

This class explores the leadership challenges that are unique to Christian ministry, and especially local churches.

*Course Objectives*

1. Students will develop a theology of evangelism.

2. Students will be able to articulate their story of becoming a follower of Christ.
3. Students will develop a personal, church, and global strategy for evangelism.
4. Students will develop an introductory understanding of ecclesiology, church health, being able to explain and identify key aspects of church health.

***Course Procedures:***

**Texts:**
- *Jesus Driven Ministry,* by Ajith Fernando
- *The Celtic Way of Evangelism: How Christianity Can Reach the West Again,* by George G. Hunter III
- *Living Church: Convictions of a Lifelong Pastor,* by John Stott
- *Christian Mission in the Modern World,* by John Stott

**Pre-class Assignment (due on the first day of class):**
All papers should be double spaced, 12-point, Times New Roman font, with standard margins and proper citations.

**1. Read**
Read all of the assigned texts before our first class session. Be prepared to discuss. You will be asked to sign a document verifying that you read the texts on the first day of class.

**2. Reflect**
Write a 1-page reflection paper for each of the text books (4 papers total). Include:

a. A summary of the main point of the book
b. A main takeaway from each book

c. A point of controversy (if any) from the book
   d. 3 main questions the book should make a pastor ask about his or her own ministry

   Be prepared to discuss your paper with the rest of the class.

## 3. Reflect

Write a 2-page reflection paper describing your process of becoming a follower of Christ with the intention of sharing your faith in Christ with a nonbeliever. Be prepared to share this with the rest of the class.

## 4. Evangelism Case Study

Write a 2-page reflective case study.
   Please do four things:
   a. Describe a time when you tried to share Christ with another person. Provide adequate details to illuminate the situation (but feel free to change names and other details as you think is appropriate), and what happened with the person.
   b. Describe how you chose to approach the person and why.
   c. Describe how you think you *should* have responded based on the books we read for this class (whether that is how you responded initially or not).
   d. Bring enough copies of the case study for yourself, your classmates, and the instructor. We will discuss the case study in class.

* All case studies will be confidential, and all copies will be returned to the author at the end of our discussion.

**Post-class Assignment:**
Write a 4-page paper on Evangelism and/or Church Health

> We will discuss possible topics for this paper in greater detail in class, but you will write a 4-page paper on a topic of your own choosing within the topics covered in your reading, lectures, and classroom discussion. Examples of potential topics include (but are not limited to):
>
> - A strategy for personal evangelism / A strategy for church evangelism / A strategy for church planting / A strategy for church revitalization / A theology of church health. *(Dunmire, 2015)*

## Indiana Wesleyan University, Marion, Indiana
### IWU: Religion 275 Evangelism and Global Outreach

This course examines the history of missions and outreach movements beginning with biblical times to the present. Attention is given to both the historical patterns which shaped outreach endeavors as well as the several methodologies which have been and are being used by various outreach organizations.

Goals of this class include instilling and knowledge of the principles of evangelism, a commitment to evangelism and outreach, and the skills necessary to be an efficient evangelist.

Books required for this course are:

- *Becoming a Contagious Christian*, by Bill Hybels and Mark Middelburg
- *True Story: A Christianity Worth Believing In*, by James Choung
- *Soul Shaper*, by Keith Drury

### IWU: YTH 371 Evangelism and Global Outreach Practicum

Each student will be involved in practical experiences in a local ministry setting providing the student with a 'laboratory' for the application of the principles of evangelism and global outreach as taught in the co-requisite course, Rel-275. (Rel-275 is Evangelism and Global Outreach — see above description.)

There are no textbooks for this course. This class is taken at the same time as Religion 275, and is a practical hands-on application of the classwork. Students work in a local church-based ministry. They are expected to participate in at least one worship service at their assigned church for ten weeks, and, in addition, must engage in their ministry assignment for a minimum of two hours per week. The student and their ministry supervisor must complete a monthly report and then students share in class the experiences and insights from their ministry assignment.

**IWU: Religion 345 Sports Evangelism and Discipleship:**
This course explores the theoretical foundations and practical methods of evangelism and discipleship in a sports ministry context. The goal of this course is to help students understand the purpose of sports ministry, be able to defend the concept of sports ministry, understand discipleship and mentoring, explain and employ various evangelistic methods, and understand specific sports ministries such as Athletes in Action and others.

Textbooks required for this course are:

- *Sports Outreach: Principles and Practices for Successful Sports Ministry*, by Steve Conner.
- *True Story: A Christianity Worth Believing In*, by James Choung

*Note:* There is also an extensive list of books and articles that are listed as supplemental reading.

**IWU: YTH 371 Youth Evangelism and Discipleship**
This course establishes both principles and practices of evangelism and discipleship, which are uniquely applicable to persons in the second decade of Life.

The goal is to develop the foundations of youth ministry, help the student explain their understanding of the Gospel and evangelize teens, understand the methodologies of evangelism, make the student familiar with literature on youth evangelism and discipleship, and develop a comprehensive youth ministry.

Textbooks required for this course are:

- *Sticky Faith, Youth Worker Edition*, by Kara Powell, Brad Griffin and Cheryl Crawford
- *Soul Shaper*, by Keith Drury

Supplemental reading includes multiple articles and online chapters. Other recommended reading includes:

- *Becoming a Contagious Christian*, by Bill Hybels and Mark Mittleburg
- *Awakening Youth Discipleship* by Brian Mahan, Michael Warren and David White
- *Almost Christian*, by Kenda Dean
- *Discipleship*, by Dietrich Bonhoeffer
- *Simple Student Ministry*, by Eric Geiger and Jeff Borton
- *Relationships Unfiltered*, by Andrew Root *(Wuertley, 2015)*

# Kingswood University, Sussex, New Brunswick, Canada
## KU: Personal Evangelism, CE 209

### Course Description
Personal Evangelism is not intended to be just another course. It is to be an experience. There will be time spent in the classroom. There will be theory and teaching. "However," the professor says, "it is my prayer that the Holy Spirit will move us out of the classroom to lead people to Christ."

### Course Rationale
All Christians are evangelists — there is no choice in this. The choice we have is to be effective or ineffective — good or bad evangelists. To be a good evangelist is to get so full of God that He just spills out into the lives of those around you. To be a bad evangelist is to block the flow of God, and get full of other things — doubts, fears, self-pity, pride, the world . . . anything but God. The purpose of this course is to help you be an effective evangelist.

### Course Objectives

**Cognitive . . . what you should know and understand:**
- A greater understanding of God's plan for evangelizing the world. This will include knowledge of biblical methods of evangelism, as well as evangelism throughout church history, and right now.

**Affective . . . what you should feel and appreciate:**
- A "heartbeat" for evangelism: an awareness of the tremendous need all around you, a compassion that allows Jesus to meet that need through you.

**Behavioral...what you should experience and do:**
- Set a goal — a specific number of people to lead to the Lord in the next year, as the Holy Spirit enables. Each student should lead one person to Christ during the 4 month course period.

*Course Textbooks*
- *The Bible*
- *Simple Evangelism,* by Mike MacNeil

*Course Requirements*
**Reading:**
Each student is responsible for reading three books from the bibliography or any other approved book.

**Projects:**
1. A personal reaction paper to one of the 3 books assigned for reading (1500 words)
2. A brief personal reaction paper to the place visited on your outreach (1000 words).
3. 10 written accounts of attempting to share your faith with a non-Christian.
4. Three 1/3rd-term exams

## KU: Church Health, Growth and Leadership PM 307

*Course Description*
This course examines transferable principles and practices which contribute to the health and growth of local churches & para-church organizations, focusing on Biblical and theological foundations as well as practical leadership strategies which can be applied in real life ministry situations.

*Course Rationale*

The health and growth of the church/organization becomes a central concern for every pastor and leader tasked with the responsibility to advance the work of Jesus Christ in this world. This course will assist current and prospective Christian leaders in understanding key factors related to leading culturally relevant, effective, growth & healthy churches and para-church organizations/ministries.

*Course Objectives*

**Cognitive . . . what you should know:**
- The Biblical foundations, philosophies and practices of church/ministry health and growth.
- The major factors which commonly negatively affect the vitality of the church/organizations.
- How to turn a declining ministry into a healthy/growing ministry.

**Affective . . . what you should feel and appreciate:**
- God's burden for reaching the lost, and being a redemptive influence in society.
- Passion, confidence and excitement for leading growing, vibrant churches and ministries.
- Unease for accepting the status quo (plateaued and declining churches/ministries).

**Behavioral . . . what you should experience and be able to do:**
- Craft strategies and structures for leading vibrant, healthy, growing churches and ministries.
- Articulate the principles, practices and philosophies of a healthy/growing ministry.

*Evangelism Training*

- Wisely implement church health and growth principles and practices.

## Course Textbooks
1. *The Book of Church Growth*, by Thom Rainer
2. *Natural Church Development*, by Christian Schwartz
3. *The 21 Irrefutable Laws of Leadership*, by John Maxwell

**Reading Reports:**

a. ***Book of Church Growth:***
Read only chapters 1 — 7, and 17 — 31. Choose 4 chapters (between chapters 17-30) and prepare a 6 page report (1.5 pgs. x 4 chapters.) summarizing the chapters, and offering personal reflections on the principle/practice; what they mean; and the implications of these church health/growth principles to yourself and your future ministries.

b. ***21 Irrefutable Laws:***
Read any 10 chapters in the book (your choice). Choose 2 of the laws, and prepare two 1-page summaries of what the law states, how well these leadership principles are presently integrated into your life, and how you could improve these leadership principles in your own life & ministry. Identify two leaders you personally know, who either positively or negatively exemplify these leadership principles.

**Church Visit:**
Students, working in teams of 2, will visit a church/synagogue/mosque for a public worship service that is *significantly* different than the type of church where they typically worship.

The purpose of the exercise is to gain sensitivity to what a first time 'visitor' to the churches you attend or lead, may feel as they come to worship. Students will discuss their visit and jointly submit a 3 - 4 page summary of their experiences, specifically noting: the name/ place/ time of the church visit; what they felt/ internally experienced during their visit; general observations concerning the church facility, staff & worship service; does the church have a high visitor sensitivity quotient?; how could they improve their visitor sensitivity?; what aspects of the worship service/facility were out-of-the-ordinary or seemed awkward for you? Conclude the paper by reflecting on what implications this experience has to your home church (what does my local church need to do different, so as to have a positive impact/welcome on visitors). Be sure to include the names of both students on the cover page.

**Welcome, Follow-up & Integration Plan:**
Develop a culturally relevant, strategic plan for welcoming, gathering contact information from guests, following up, and integrating new people into the life and ministries of the local church.

*Project:*

Church Health/Growth Case Study & Presentation:

> Students, working in teams of 2 or 3, will select one local church (*other than your home churches*) and conduct a church health/growth analysis based on *Schwarz's 8 Principles* and our classroom lectures. Conduct face-to-face interviews with *at least* 2 of the church's leaders and your own observations of the

church's ministry. Report: 6 pages & a 10 min. class presentation. Identify the strengths & weaknesses of the church; the church's growth potential; the leadership strengths/weakness of the pastor/leadership team; effectiveness of its evangelism & welcome/integration programs; observable limiting factors affecting the church, etc. Include a prescription of 3 recommendations the church should implement to make the biggest difference in the health/growth potential of the church.

**Proposed Course Outline:**
The class chooses 2 or 3 topics from the list below

*Church Health/Growth*
- Problem of Declining Attendance
- Identifying Limiting Factors
- The issue of Soil Conditions
- Principles of Church Growth
- Pastoral Tenure
- Lay Involvement/Empowerment
- Staffing for Success
- Vision & Strategies
- Evolving Infrastructure & Roles
- Men's Ministry Emphasis
  Effective Evangelism & Entry Points
- Role of Preaching
- Welcome, Follow up & Integration
- Worship Experiences
- Advertising
- Drawing the Net

## Leadership
- Leadership Overview
- Academic Insights
- When Leader's Fail
- First Things First
- Team Building
- Fundraising
- Making Tough Calls
- Delegation of Authority

## Evangelism
- Sports Evangelism
- Crusade Evangelism
- Apologetics Evangelism
- Community Saturation
- Family Evangelism
- Program Evangelism
- Power Evangelism
- Child Evangelism
- Support Group Evangelism

# KU: Empowering and Equipping Lay Ministry PM 312

## Course Description
An exploration of the importance of lay ministry, and the skills and philosophies involved in identifying, developing, supporting and deploying lay persons for effective ministry.

## Course Rationale
The task of empowering persons for ministry requires an "equipping ministry paradigm," skills in coaching/mentoring,

and knowledge of the systems available for the implementation of this process.

## Course Objectives

**Cognitive ... as a result of this course the student should know and understand:**
- Biblical mandates and importance of "lay ministry" and "the priesthood of believers."
- Skills required to equip and support lay persons in ministry.
- Value of identifying, developing and deploying lay people by their spiritual gifts/passions.

**Affective ... as a result of this course, the student should feel and appreciate:**
- A passion for lay equipping ministry.
- The value of multiplying a local church's ministry through effective lay ministry.

**Behavioral ... as a result of this course, the student should be able to:**
- Identify the spiritual gifts/passions of lay people.
- Implement systems to equip/develop persons for lay ministry.
- Release and support lay people into effective ministry responsibilities.

## Course Textbooks
- *The Lay Ministry Revolution,* by Eddy Hall
- *Unfinished Business,* by Greg Ogden

*Course Requirements*
**Readings:**
1. Textbook: *The Lay Ministry Revolution* by Eddy Hall & Gary Morsch
2. Textbook: *Unfinished Business* by Greg Ogden
3. Collateral Reading

Read a total of 200 pages from a minimum of 3 books on any topic relative to developing and implementing a strong emphasis on lay ministry (read selected chapters from a variety of books listed in the bibliography, on aspects of lay-ministry you wish to understand better). Report the names of the books, authors, number of pages read, 2 or 3 best insights, and personal reflections

## KU: Pastoral Ministry PM 400

*Course Description*

This course studies the work and responsibilities of the pastor (with the exception of work associated with the preparation and delivery of sermons). The student will be introduced to a broad range of pastoral functions, duties and skills, with opportunities to learn through instruction, practice, observation, discussion and interaction with guest pastors/lecturers and site visits to leading edge churches.

*Course Textbooks*

- *Leadership Handbook of Preaching and Worship,* by James D. Berkley (General Editor)
- *Practical Guide for Pastoral Ministry,* by Stan Toler

- *Wesleyan Pastor's Manual*, Wesleyan Publishing House or the Pastor's Manual for the student's own home denomination. There are no specific reading requirements, just an important resource.

*Collateral Reading:*

Read *selected chapters* from 2 or more books on *any* topics you sense you need to understand better (a TOTAL of 100 pages). Two highly recommended (but not required books) are *Dangerous Calling,* by Paul Tripp OR *Leading from the Second Chair,* by Mike Bonem. 1 page Summary and Reflection Report of the reading.

*Ministry Assignments:*
**Visitation Ministry.**
Write a portion of the paper in a *'verbatim'* fashion. Reference the class hand-out notes on 'pastoral visitation'. Write a 2 - 3 page *Reflection Paper* for each of the 2 visits made utilizing the guidelines listed below. Note: you may visit people alone or in teams of 2, but submit your papers, individually.

1. Non-Relative Pastoral Visit:
   Visit a person you are not related to, such as an elderly person in his/her home, or in a nursing home, or visit a hospitalized (medical or psychiatric), or incarcerated person (prison or detention center). This assignment may be done alone or in pairs, or with a Sussex area pastor, or with your home church pastor during school break.

2. Evangelism Visit:
   Attempt to talk to a person who does not yet know Jesus as Lord and Savior, about their spiritual condition. This visit may take place in any location, such as: mall, home visit, prison, hospital, etc.

**Visitation Ministry**
(private home or nursing home or hospital or prison; and evangelism)

1. Name of person visited, place and date, and circumstance of visit

2. Preparation for the visit (what did you do before hand)
   a. How did you intentionally arrange to meet this person?
   b. What were you feeling and thinking prior to meeting the individual?
   c. List your steps or procedure of preparation for the visit. (i.e. Did you read or review anything? Did you take literature with you to leave with the person?)
   d. Share 'word for word' one 'interesting' aspect of your conversation.
   e. Other than 'fulfilling a classroom assignment', what did you hope to accomplish with this visit?

3. Evaluation of the visit
- To what extent was the "purpose" of the visit realized?
- List 6 things that pleased you/surprised you/ disappointed you about the visit.
- List 3 pastoral visitation concepts you learned, how they will be helpful in your ministry.

# Oklahoma Wesleyan University, Bartlesville, Oklahoma
## OKWU: Evangelism PAMI 2113

*Course Description*

A study of and training in the philosophy and methodologies of evangelism, especially in our secular, post-modern cultural milieu. The goal of this course is to assist the student in developing an understanding of and the skills for both pursuing personal lifestyle evangelism and also implementing evangelism within the context of the local church by reflecting on one's own faith journey, by reading and reflecting on various texts, and by actively practicing the developing of spiritual friendships.

*Learning Outcomes*

1. Develop and learn how to articulate a personal philosophy and understanding of evangelism; a philosophy that is both biblically sound and approachable in daily living within the current, post-modern age and their ministry context.
2. Develop a biblically informed strategic evangelistic methods.
3. Increase their awareness to the perspectives of unchurched people.
4. Look at new ways to reach people in the 21st Century (Post-Modern context).
5. Discern the difference between gathering and going evangelistic methodology.
6. Grasp the importance of engaging culture through social action for increased evangelistic effectiveness.

7. Understand the importance of church planting in the infiltration of the world for Christ.
8. Heighten their knowledge that evangelism is not simply winning people to Christ, but connecting them to a faith community through intentional discipleship.
9. Deepen their passion for the mission of the church of going and making disciples.

**By the end of the semester the student will . . .**
1. Discover and learn how to articulate his/her personal philosophy and understanding of evangelism; a philosophy that is both biblically sound and approachable in daily living within the current, post-modern age and their ministry context.
2. Understand the basic historical watershed "events" that have led to the secularization of western culture and the advent of post-modernism.
3. Recognize and become acquainted with the ideals, values, mentality, and actions of living in both a modern and a post-modern Worldview.
4. Know and understand a process/model of how persons make the spiritual decision to believe in the message of the Gospel and to follow Jesus in their personal lives.
5. Gain a cursory acquaintance with the dynamics of church planting as the most effective means of evangelism.
6. Become conversant with the major objections to Christianity and learn how to debunk and engage them with items consistent with both a Modern and Post-Modern context.
7. Become conversant with the missional Church.

**Textbooks required for this course are:**
- *The Surge: Churches Catching the Wave of Christ's Love for the Nations*, by Pete Briscoe.
- *Master Plan of Evangelism*, by Robert Coleman
- Other articles and videos as assigned within Bb LMS (Learning Management System)

**Class Delivery**
Classes will utilize various teaching methods and scaffolding techniques: lectures, interactive discussion of assigned readings, videos, guest lecturer(s) in the form of videos, small group presentations, and "on-the-job" assignments. There will be several writing experiences for the student throughout the semester—written book reviews for each of the textbooks, and three brief personal evangelism reports. In addition to the textbooks, the student will occasionally be required to read selected articles on evangelism.

This class will be offered in a blended format with the use of Bb, which means that while both class sessions will be face to face, other class discussion will conducted online. Students need to plan on being online between 1-2 hours a week by posting and responding to the instructor and their classmates. 10% participation grade will be assessed for online posts and regularly participation.

**Interviews with non-Christian/un-churched people.**
Conduct an interview with an unbelieving/unchurched friend, neighbor, co-worker, relative or stranger. NOTE: A classmate or fellow college student who only attends church sporadically does not count. The point of this assignment is to get you out of your comfort zone and begin to build friendships with others. For this exercise, it is okay to explain clearly to the

individual that this is simply a 15-20 minute interview and it is a requirement for one of your university classes. Remember that all answers are voluntary and confidential, although you must write a brief paper regarding your experiences and answers from the interview. Approach the interview with sensitivity, openness and a gracious spirit. The use of Internet chat rooms is not permitted. We will discuss your experience in class. With the exception of the final report, these reports should be 600 to 750 words in length. Please describe your reaction to the interview.

Some suggested questions to be asked (Please ask at least six questions)

1. How would you define God?
2. Ask the 6 Worldview Questions.
3. Can a person know God (How?)
4. Who was/is Jesus Christ?
5. What is the biggest problem, in your opinion facing humankind today?
6. What is (how do you define) sin?
7. How do you feel about the church (or Christianity) and why do you feel this way?
8. How would you define having a relationship with Jesus Christ?
9. Do you think there is only one way to reach God? (Elaborate)
10. What happens after we die?
11. How would you define a Christian?
12. Can a person get to heaven? If yes, how?
13. What is your philosophy of life?
14. What do you think is common to world religions? How do they differ?

**Day of Evangelism:**
This is where the rubber meets the road. Meet at OKWU at 11am for a trip to University of Tulsa (TU) for an opportunity to put into practice what you have been learning by sharing your faith. We will meet afterwards at Dr. Smith's house for dinner and a debrief session. Submit at least a two page reflection on the day. Please be sure to include the following in your reflection:
- Key ideas and thoughts that you learned from this exercise
- How your view of evangelism has changed as a result of the day of evangelism
- What you wish you would have said/done differently
- What helped prepare you for this day.
- What would it take to be committed to a life of evangelism?

**Personal Philosophy of Evangelism/Discipleship:**
- Your final paper is expected to be 10-12 pages in length (including title page and works cited page). Your paper should use class notes, textbooks and other documented resources. The MLA Handbook is the standard guide for writing papers.
- You are faced with one of two possible challenges: (1) You have decided to start a new ministry within today's post-modern's context or (2) You are transitioning your present more modern oriented ministry to reach people in today's post-modern context.
- Outline your understanding of your mission field. Include what ministry context you see yourself in (lead pastor, singles, college, youth, young career, cross-cultural ministry).

- Include in your paper:
  - Your understanding of the gospel, conversion, discipleship, sanctification, in your specific context (be sure to cite authors and scripture to help you state your case).
  - Core values and convictions of the ministry.
  - Evangelism/Discipleship strategy.
  - Share how you will not only "bring them in" but also "raise them up" be sure to list methods and steps you plan to utilize.
  - What particular challenges and opportunities do you foresee?
  - Your definition of success after a five-year run of ministry.
  - How you will include healing and prayer in terms of evangelism.

## Southern Wesleyan University, Central, South Carolina
### SWU: Religion 3103: Evangelism and Church Health

This course is an introduction to the Biblical foundations, guidelines and challenges to effective personal and corporate evangelism. Attention is given to understanding the culture, the conversion experience, and the missional nature of the believer and the church. Strategies for local church growth and participating in outreach and evangelism are explored.

**Textbooks required for this course are:**
- Just *Walk Across the Room*, by Bill Hybels
- *Purple Fish*, by Mark Wilson
- *An Unstoppable Force*, by Erwin McManus

Students must write out their own personal testimony, do a 14 day prayer project based on the one in *Just Walk Across the Room* by Hybels or do three of the "fishing tips" in Wilson's book, participate in at least two intentional witnessing experiences, do a journal through the book of Acts, participate in an out of class meeting with the professor to discuss spiritual growth and lifestyle change, and develop and submit a 1,200 word personal philosophy on the missional nature and lifestyle of the Christian believer as a capstone assignment to the class.

## Fellowship of Leaders Acquiring Ministerial Education (Flame)

Flame, the Fellowship of Leaders Acquiring Ministerial Education, is a ministerial preparation program of the Wesleyan Church. Participants attend conferences and follow up by doing post-class work.

The syllabus for each Flame evangelism course is determined by the individual teacher. One example below was developed by Reverend Michael Black from Williamston, Michigan.

**Textbooks:**
- *Evangelism Handbook* by Alvin Reid
- Any 200 page book on evangelism, revival or church planting of their choice.
- *The Diary of David Brainerd* found online

Each class participant is given an assortment of projects to do, several papers to write, in-church classes to conduct, interviews to conduct, and hands-on witnessing opportunities. This is not an easy class and there is much that students are assigned both in-class and post-class. *(Black, 2015)*

CHAPTER 8

# Best Evangelism Resources

While a recommended selection of the best evangelism resources is as varied as the number of people with whom you check, here is a list of titles that seem to rise to the top:

## Personal Evangelism: Classics

*Becoming a Contagious Christian*
Bill Hybels and Mark Mittelberg
Zondervan, ISBN 978-0310210085
Amazon Description: You will discover your own natural evangelism style, how to develop a contagious Christian character, to build spiritually strategic relationships, to direct conversations toward matters of faith, and to share biblical truths in everyday language.

*Just Walk Across the Room*
Bill Hybels
Zondervan, ISBN 978-0310494157
Amazon Description: Building on the solid foundation laid in *Becoming a Contagious Christian*, Bill Hybels shows how you can participate in the model first set by Jesus, who stepped down from heaven 2,000 years ago to bring hope and redemption to broken people living in a fallen world.

***Out of the Salt Shaker and Into the World***
Rebecca Pippert
IVP Books, ISBN 978-0830822201
Amazon Description: Through stories, biblical insight and plain common sense, Pippert helps us feel relaxed and enthusiastic about sharing our faith. She offers an inspiring view of what effective, engaging evangelism might look like—for individuals as well as for churches through memorable stories.

***Lifestyle Evangelism***
Dr. Joe Aldrich
Multnomah Books, ISBN 978-1590527542
Amazon Description: Dr. Joe Aldrich shows us how we can build genuine, caring relationships with nonbelievers that will open their hearts to the gospel message. The author's approach is biblical, practical, and natural. *Lifestyle Evangelism* is the definitive work in introducing people to the Savior in a way that displays God's authentic love for the lost.

***Master Plan of Evangelism***
Dr. Robert Coleman
Revell, ISBN 978-0800788087
Amazon Description: For more than forty years this classic study has shown Christians how to minister to the people God brings into their lives. Instead of drawing on the latest popular fad or the newest selling technique, Dr. Robert E. Coleman looks to the Bible to find the answer to the question: What was Christ's strategy for evangelism?

## Personal Evangelism: Newer Titles

***Organic Outreach for Ordinary People: Sharing Good News Naturally***
Kevin G. Harney
Zondervan, ISBN 978-0310273950
Amazon Description: Deep in our hearts we have a burning passion to pass on the good news we have received. But, where do we start? We want to share our faith, but we don't want it to feel awkward, uncomfortable, or unnatural . . . for them or for us! *Organic Outreach for Ordinary People* will help you shape a personal approach to passing on the good news of Jesus in natural ways.

***Organic Outreach for Families: Turning Your Home into a Lighthouse***
Kevin G. Harney
Zondervan, ISBN 978-0310273974
Amazon Description: Kevin and Sherry Harney share insights from the Scriptures and give practical advice from their own experience to help you learn how to transform your home into a lighthouse of God's amazing grace.

***Purple Fish: A Heart for Sharing Jesus***
By Mark O. Wilson
Wesleyan Publishing House, ISBN 978-0898279108
Amazon description: Through amazing and often humorous stories as well as many practical suggestions, Wilson encourages the reader to rethink what it means to bring lost people to Jesus. It will leave readers saying, "I haven't thought of it that way before. I can do that!"

*Questioning Evangelism*
Randy Newman
Kregel Publications, ISBN 978-0825433245
Amazon Description: A revolutionary look at sharing Christ with unbelievers by using the probing, provocative, and penetrating method Jesus used to engage others in personal dialogue and caring interaction.

*Reimagining Evangelism*
Rick Richardson
IVP Books, ISBN 978-0830833429
Amazon Description: Imagine being free to be yourself and free for the Spirit to work in you. Imagine that it doesn't depend on you alone but that you can be an important part of a witnessing community. Imagine telling people stories instead of trying to download content. Here is your invitation to reimagine what evangelism could be for you.

*Evangelism Made Slightly Less Difficult: How to Interest People Who Aren't Interested*
Nick Pollard
IVP Books, ISBN 978-0830819089
Amazon Description: In this readable and accessible book, evangelist Nick Pollard shows how to break through the barrier of disinterest. He shows why Jesus can and should make a difference for the people you know. And he shows how you can interest them in learning more about Jesus.

### Soul Shaper: Becoming the Person God Wants You to Be
Keith Drury
Wesleyan Publishing House, ISBN 978-0898277050
Amazon Description: Master teacher Keith Drury has taken the best from his two previous classics (*Spiritual Disciplines for Ordinary People* and *With Unveiled Faces*), and powerfully concentrated and updated it into this new and accessible book, offering the wisdom of ancient disciplines in simple, practical terms that today's Christians can understand and apply.

### True Story: A Christianity Worth Believing In
James Choung
IVP, ISBN 978-0830836093
Amazon Description: Join Caleb and Anna on their spiritual journeys as they probe Christianity from inside and out. Get past the old clichés and simplistic formulas. And discover a new way of understanding and presenting the Christian faith that really matters in a broken world.

### Sticky Faith
Kara Powell and Chap Clark
Zondervan, ISBN 978-0310329329
Amazon Description: This easy-to-read guide presents both a compelling rationale and a powerful strategy to show parents how to actively encourage their children's spiritual growth so that it will stick to them into adulthood and empower them to develop a living, lasting faith.

## Basic Apologetics Books
### Case for Christ
Lee Strobel
Zondervan, ISBN 978-0310339304
Amazon Description: Strobel's tough, point-blank questions make this bestselling book read like a captivating, fast-paced novel. But it is not fiction. It is a riveting quest for the truth about history's most compelling figure.

### Case for Faith
Lee Strobel
Zondervan, ISBN 978-0310339298
Amazon Description: This Gold Medallion-winning book is for those who may be feeling attracted to Jesus but who are faced with difficult questions standing squarely in their path. For Christians, it will deepen their convictions and give them fresh confidence in discussing Christianity with even their most skeptical friends.

### Jesus Among Other Gods
Ravi Zacharias
W Publishing Group, ISBN 978-0849943270
Amazon Description: *Jesus Among Other Gods* provides the answers to the most fundamental claims about Christianity, such as: Aren't all religions fundamentally the same? Was Jesus who He claimed to be? Can one study the life of Christ and demonstrate conclusively that He was and is the way, the truth, and the life?

## *Mere Christianity*
C.S. Lewis
Harper San Francisco, ISBN 978-0060652920
Amazon Description: In the classic *Mere Christianity*, C.S. Lewis, the most important writer of the 20th century, explores the common ground upon which all of those of Christian faith stand together. Bringing together Lewis' legendary broadcast talks during World War Two from his three previous books, *Mere Christianity* provides an unequaled opportunity for believers and nonbelievers alike to hear this powerful apologetic for the Christian faith.

## Church Evangelism Books

### *No Perfect People Allowed: Creating a Come-As-You-Are Culture in the Church*
John Burke
Zondervan, ISBN 978-0310275015
Amazon Description: *No Perfect People Allowed* shows you how to deconstruct the five main barriers standing between emerging generations and your church by creating the right culture. From inspiring stories of real people once far from God, to practical ideas that can be applied by any local church, this book offers a refreshing vision of the potential and power of the Body of Christ to transform lives today.

### *Becoming a Contagious Church*
Mark Mittelberg
Zondervan, ISBN 978-0310279198
Amazon Description: *Becoming a Contagious Church* dispels outdated preconceptions and reveals evangelism as it really

can be. What's more, it walks you through a 6-Stage Process and includes a brand-new 6-Stage Process assessment tool for taking your church beyond mere talk to infectious energy, action, and lasting commitment.

### Surprising Insights from the Unchurched and Proven Ways to Reach Them

Thom Rainer

Zondervan, ISBN 978-0310286134

Amazon Description: Filled with charts, graphs, and other visual aids, plus an abundance of true-life accounts, this book explodes myths about the unchurched. You will discover:
- Why pastors and doctrinal preaching are critical
- The enormous influence of family and relationships
- Which things matter more than we thought, and which matter less
- The traits of unchurched-reaching leaders
- How to become a church for the unchurched

### Organic Outreach for Churches: Infusing Evangelistic Passion in Your Local Congregation

Kevin G. Harney

Zondervan, ISBN 978-0310273967

Amazon Description: This book is a roadmap for pastors and leaders who wish to infuse evangelistic passion into every aspect of their church's life.

CHAPTER 9

# Evangelism Awards

The only evangelism awards that were discovered are the *Harry Denman Distinguished Evangelism Award* and the *Culture of the Call Church Award*, both of which are given each year by the United Methodist Church. These awards are presented by the Foundation for Evangelism located in Lake Junaluska, North Carolina. The stated mission of the Foundation for Evangelism is "to promote, encourage and provide resources for responsible evangelism, enable The United Methodist Church to bring persons into a personal relationship with Jesus Christ." This organization, in addition to presenting the annual Distinguished Evangelism Award, funds professors and educators in Methodist-affiliated and Wesleyan tradition seminaries throughout the world. *(Honoring Excellence in Evangelism, 2014)*

The *Culture of the Call Church Award* "annually recognizes one local United Methodist Congregation with a culture that encourages young people to respond to God's call to full-time Christian service as a result of their being active in the life of that church. The Foundation for Evangelism, as part of its vision to raise up generations of leaders with a passion for evangelism, awards this honor to highlight throughout the denomination the outstanding work being done in the local church." The 2015 award winner was the Hastings, Minnesota, UMC. *(Honoring Excellence in Evangelism, 2014)*

The *Harry Denman Evangelism Award* is given annually

to a member of the United Methodist clergy or laity who has been nominated by persons within the United Methodist Church and is presented at the United Methodist Clergy, Laity and Youth Conference. The nomination forms are on-line at foundationforevangelism.org. The nominator must identify themselves, explain how long the person has served as a pastor, deacon or ordained United Methodist, give examples of the nominee's effectiveness in evangelism, provide a biography of the nominee, and describe how the nominee embodies the passion of the foundation and the church. Nominations are then reviewed and a winner is selected. There is a separate form for clergy and laity. This award is presented to clergy, laity and youth.

Past winners of this award have included:

- 2014: Bishop Richard Looney, Chattanooga, TN
- 2013: Rev. R Mark Beeson, Granger, IN
- 2012: Rev. Charles Anderson, San Antonio, TX
- 2011: Dr. Ed Robb, The Woodlands, TX
- 2010: Rev. Shane Bishop, Fairview, IL
- 2009: Rev. Jeorge Acevedo, Cape Coral, FL
- 2008: Dr. Keith Tonkel, Jackson, MS
- 2007: Dr. Kent Millard, Indianapolis, IN
- 2006: Dr. Norman Neaves, Oklahoma City, OK
- 2005: Dr. George E. Morris, Canton, GA
- 2004: Ms. Billie Fidlin, Phoenix, AZ
- 2003: Rev. Dr. Michael Slaughter, Tipp City, OH

CHAPTER 10

# Evangelism Training Centers and Conferences in the United States

## Evangelism Training Centers

### Liberty University, Master of Arts Christian Ministry — Evangelism and Church Planting

In this Master of Arts program, the student studies evangelism practices and church planting methods in courses such as Spiritual Factors of Growing Churches, Introduction to Church Planting, and Evangelism and the Growing Church. This degree can be obtained on-line. Liberty University claims to be the world's largest Christian university. *(Liberty University Master of Arts in Christian Ministry, 2015)*

### Billy Graham School of Evangelism Online

This is a 4-course study in evangelism run by the Billy Graham Evangelistic Association. It gives the student practical strategies for proclamation evangelism, with an emphasis in evangelistic preaching, and preparing the church for follow-up with new believers. The student has 180 days to finish the courses once they are signed up. Within each lesson, students are free to move back and forth between activities within that course, but are required to finish the current lesson's quiz before moving on to the next lesson. *(School of Evangelism Online, n.d.)*

### The School of Biblical Evangelism

This course was developed by Kirk Cameron and Ray Comfort. The School of Biblical Evangelism (SoBE) is an online Bible School, dedicated to training men and women to proclaim the Gospel of Jesus Christ. The school was established in 2001 by Living Waters Ministries. Through 101 online lessons, including audios, articles, and videos, students are challenged to have a biblical worldview. Each lesson is designed to equip the students to defend the historic Christian faith. The course takes approximately six months to complete. Total students since inception is 14,000 enrolled/completed. *(School of Biblical Evangelism, n.d.)*

### The Billy Graham School of Missions, Evangelism and Ministry at Southern Baptist Theological Seminary

This school offers a degree in Evangelism and Missions. The Billy Graham School combines biblical training and missionary strategy to train students to develop a vision for the lost and the tools they need to fulfill the vision of spreading the gospel in its full biblical integrity to every person and every people group in North America and around the world. They offer a Master of Divinity, including a Master in Church Planting and in International Church Planting. They also offer a Master of Arts in Missiology, as well as a Diploma in Missions. *(Department of Evangelism and Missions, 2015)*

### Billy Graham Center for Evangelism, Wheaton College

The BGCE is committed to developing and mobilizing Jesus-followers to share their faith winsomely and wisely. They do this by training and resourcing leaders and lay Christians to develop a lifestyle of evangelism.

The BGCE offers a Master in Evangelism and Leadership which is designed to equip the student to think critically and act creatively to communicate the gospel and lead the change that's needed in a contemporary, multi-ethnic world. The school offers the option to complete the Master in Evangelism and Leadership degree in several formats. These formats include full time resident students, and a combination of full-time or part-time, including both on-campus and off-campus options. *(BGCE at Wheaton College, n.d.)*

## Evangelism Conferences

### Organic Outreach International

The Organic Outreach International Conference was begun in 2011 by Dr. Kevin Harney, Senior Pastor of Shoreline Community Church in Monterrey, California. Dr. Harney is also the author of the *Organic Outreach* books. In the past several years, the organization has expanded their slate to include many on-line materials as well as books and live conferences.

The Organic Outreach International Conference consists of two levels. The first level is called Intensive Training. This is a 2-day session for church leaders. Within the Intensive Training are two tracks; one for local church leaders and the second is for national and international leaders, with some of the sessions conducted together and some separate. The 2016 Intensive Training Conference included the following sessions:

- Session 1: The Law of Love
- Session 2: The Outreach Influence Team
- Session 3: The One and Two Degree Rules
- Session 4: Demonstration of Full Team Meetings
- Session 5: Demonstration of 1 on 1 and Cluster Meetings
- Session 6: Six Levels of Influence
- Session 7: Mind Shifts
- Session 8: The Gospel — Levels and Intensity
- Session 9: The Power of Innovation
- Session 10: Stories and 1$^{st}$ Year Plan

The second level is the larger Organic Outreach Conference. This is a 3-day gathering for church leaders, international and national leaders, and laypeople immediately following the Intensive Training. It consists of large group sessions of up to 800-plus people, and smaller breakout elective sessions. The November 2016, large group sessions included the following:

**Speakers and Topics**
- Kevin Harney:
  *Scattering Together*
- Nabeel Qureshi:
  *What is This Seed we Scatter?*
- Chris Brown:
  *Keeping the Right Perspective*
- Sherry Harney:
  *Strengthening the Scatterer*
- Lon Allison, Rick Richardson, Beth Seversen:
  *Transforming Your Local Church into a Scattering Movement on Mission*

- Lon Allison:
  *Scattering Love, Grace and Truth*
- Beth Seversen:
  *Scattering to Cross Boarders*
- Joshua Ryan Butler:
  *Scattering Against the Wind*
- Kevin Harney:
  *Sacrificial Scattering*
- Nabeel Qureshi:
  *Why We Scatter Seed There*

In addition to the main sessions, there were 9 "tracks" each participant could choose from during the breakout sessions. These breakouts were facilitated by the main session speakers, and by other church leaders. The breakout tracks for the November, 2016, conference were:

- Organic Outreach Selected Topics
- Scattering Seeds Through Faith and Science
- Scattering Seeds in a Resistant Culture
- Transforming Your Church Toward Evangelism Impact and Growth
- Scattering Seeds to the Church
- Organic Outreach for Ordinary People
- Outreach Workshop
- Scatter
- Loving Stronger Leaders to Stronger Outreach

For more information on the Organic Outreach Conferences, including dates for future conferences, go to www.organicoutreachconference.com or contact Walt Bennett, Executive Pastor of Organic Outreach International at walt@organicoutreach.org or 831-655-0100.

CHAPTER 11

# Evangelism Practices of Selected Churches

With a desire to discover what some of the leading churches within the Wesleyan Church are doing to promote evangelism, we emailed surveys to selected pastors based on their Conversion and Baptism figures during the 2014 ministry year. We asked them several questions;

1. Does your church use a formalized evangelism program?
2. If yes, which one do you use?
3. If no, do you use a hybrid program of your own?
4. How is this program working for you?
5. Briefly describe how the typical person finds Jesus Christ as Savior at your church.

The churches surveyed ranged in Sunday morning attendance of over 16,000 to about 900. We also tried to include a variety of geographical locations. The responding churches included those who have multiple campuses as well as those who have a single campus operation.

Most of the responding churches do not use a formalized evangelism program; although a few do currently, or have in the past. What was universal, however, was a deep-rooted evangelism culture within the church. This was evident by their responses to our questions, but also from their website information. We have included selected information from each church's website.

Almost all of the responding churches had a strong small group program as an important part of their church culture.

The churches responding to our request for information were:

- 12Stone Church, Greater Atlanta, GA
- Celebrate Community Church, Sioux Falls, SD
- Fountain Springs Church, Rapid City, SD
- Kings Valley Wesleyan, New Brunswick, Canada
- Lifestream Church, Allendale, MI
- New Hope Church, Durham, NC
- Red Cedar Church, Rice Lake, WI
- Skyline Wesleyan Church, La Mesa, CA

## 12STONE CHURCH, Lawrenceville, GA

**Wesleyan District:**
South Coastal

**Lead Pastor:**
Rev. Kevin Myers

**Web Site:**
https://12stone.com/

**Weekend Attendance (2014):**
16,278

**Locations:**
9 locations
- Central Campus. 1322 Buford Road, Lawrenceville, GA (4 Sunday services)
- Hamilton Mill. 3858 Braselton Hwy, Buford, GA (4 Sunday services)
- Flowery Branch. 4256 Martin Road, Flowery Branch, GA (4 Sunday services)
- Sugarloaf. 2050 Sugarloaf Circle, Duluth, GA (3 Sunday services)
- Bethlehem. 1000 Haymon Morris Road, Winder, GA (2 Sunday services)
- Braselton. 4500 Braselton Highway, Hoschton, GA (2 Sunday services)
- Buford. 918 Buford Hwy, Buford, GA (2 Sunday services)
- Grayson. 3425 Loganville Hwy, Loganville, GA (2 Sunday services)

- Snellville. 1255 Dogwood Road, Snellville, GA (2 Sunday services)

**2014 Ministry Year Conversions and Baptisms:**
- Conversions: 5,238
- Baptisms: 844

**Survey Responses:**

Does your church use a formalized evangelism program?

*No.*

If no, do you use a hybrid program of your own?

*For us Evangelism isn't a thing we do, but why we exist. It is core to our mission of reaching the lost, serving the least, and raising up leaders. We don't have a program for Evangelism. We don't have an Evangelism Pastor. We view every Pastor as an Evangelism Pastor. Even our Outreach Pastor, who focuses locally, oversees our community partnerships. We have a lean ministry model, so we don't do much through programs. We do focus a lot on serving and small groups.*

*We view every Pastor and every Christ Follower as having a role in Evangelism. Evangelism and reaching the lost is core to our mission and flows heavily from our Senior Pastor's heart. We design weekend services with the unchurched in mind. We pray regularly and fervently for lost people. We cast vision for our people to invest in relationships, invite people to church, and include them into the life of the church. In nearly every sermon series we* will have a salvation weekend, meaning we will have some form of inviting people to respond to the gospel. Often this could be a "come forward" or "stand in the room." We like to give our people an easy excuse to invite people to church. That's led us to creative pushes like doing our At the Movies series. This is a high invite season for us and people love to invite unchurched friends and neighbors.

For the past few years we've followed a God prompt to have an open baptism. For many this was their salvation response. While we see large numbers respond during these weekends we frequently baptize people throughout the year. We will make room for a baptism almost any Sunday. We take a couple minutes for a pastor to summarize a person's testimony then we celebrate their life change and baptism. We recognize that the baptisms and stories of life change remind our church why we exist, and we have developed a culture that highly celebrates this. We regularly cast the vision that ONE MATTERS! Baptisms carry this value and vision.

How is this program working for you?

We continue to see God bringing people to salvation and responding through baptism. God's kind favor is something we seek to steward well and fuel through prayer and dependence on him.

Briefly describe how the typical person finds Jesus Christ as Savior at your church:

The typical person comes to Sunday services. They decide to keep coming and check it out at their pace.

*The typical seeker sits through multiple weekends with salvation response opportunities before they actually respond themselves.*

**Note:**

With 25 services spread over 9 campuses in and around the Atlanta metro area, 12Stone Church is a thriving, rapidly growing urban church with a strong evangelism outreach. Their website contains this mission statement: "At 12Stone, we give ourselves away so you will experience excellence and the love of God." Their stated purpose is this: "12Stone exists so future generations will know the rescuing hand of God. "

12Stone has a strong small group ministry. Their groups meet on a 12-week semester basis to allow people an easy start and finish point. This also allows participants to explore and join different groups throughout the year. 12Stone also has a program called *Discover Faith*. This is a safe, conversational, 4-week small group where participants are encouraged to explore elements of the Christian life like salvation, prayer, the Bible and worship. A link to this program is found at https://12stone.com/discoverfaith/. There is a 60-page downloadable participant guide included at this link.

# CELEBRATE COMMUNITY CHURCH, Sioux Falls, South Dakota

*Wesleyan District:*

Northwest

*Lead Pastor:*

Dr. Keith Allen Loy

*Web Site:*

www.celebratesf.org

*Weekend Attendance (2014):*

4,174

*Locations:*

3 locations

- Sycamore Campus. 1000 S. Sycamore Ave, Sioux Falls, SD (3 weekend services)
- Meadows Campus. 3211 Shirley Ave, Sioux Falls, SD (3 weekend services)
- Branden Campus. 201 West Park St., Branden, SD (2 weekend services)

*2014 Ministry Year Conversions and Baptisms:*

- Conversions: 881
- Baptisms: 281

*Survey Responses:*

Does your church use a formalized evangelism program?

> *We do not use a formal evangelism program. Rather it is a part of everything we talk about. Some examples are, "The guest is the most important person," "Jesus saw people, had compassion, saw their need," "Constantly encouraging people to invite," "Sharing stories of people who have come to know Christ," etc. It's a part of our ongoing language.*

If no, do you use a hybrid program of your own?

> *Our vision statement is that Celebrate is "Devoted to BUILDING RELATIONSHIPS that grow thousands of people in Christ, toward the fulfillment of the Great Commission." Everything we do is about building relationships. It is something we talk about all the time. Our core values are: Welcome, Worship, Word. The most important is WELCOME. We always talk about it and look at how we can improve. "Truth can't be expressed until Trust is experienced." It all comes back into the relationship.*

Briefly describe how the typical person finds Jesus Christ as Savior at your church:

> *It will sound like repetition, but everything happens through a personal relationship with a Celebrate member, who loves the person unconditionally, and through that relationship is invited to attend the service where they are welcomed home. It is through this relationship with people that they find their relationship with Jesus.*

**Note:**

Celebrate Community Church has a dynamic small group program that they call Life Groups, consisting of 94 groups for every life-stage. For example, they have one that is called an Executive Group which is specifically for business owners. Another group is for empty nesters, which meets at 6:30 AM on Thursdays. Still other groups are designated for specific life-stages like 20 to 30 somethings, blended families, single dads, divorce care, and numerous others. There are groups for runners and groups for service, as well as other interests. The church web site includes a map showing the meeting location of each group.

This statement about their groups is included under their interactive Life Group page on the Celebrate Community web site: "LIFE Groups are groups of 6-10 people who gather together for purpose of fellowship and growth in Christ. We also like to say that LIFE Groups are how we 'do life together.' Others may call their groups 'Bible studies', 'community groups' or 'small groups'. We refer to our groups as LIFE Groups because we believe that every group at Celebrate Church should bring life to you!

**LIFE Groups have 4 things in common:**
**L = LOVE** — LIFE Groups help us grow deeper in our Love for God and His Word

**I = INVITE** — LIFE Groups understand that healthy things grow and growth will happen through relationships. Personal invitations are the best way for groups to grow. LIFE Groups should always stay focused on the vision of "reaching thousands for Christ."

**F = FAMILY** — LIFE Groups provide Living Room environments to help people develop deeper relationships with people. As our love for God grows, so should our love for people.

**E = EXPERIENCE GOD** — LIFE Groups know that the best way to experience God is through fellowship with other believers. Through group members being salt and light, we can help thousands experience God through LIFE groups."

More information about Celebrate Community Church's Life Groups can be found at www.celebratesf.org/am/lifegroups.php

# FOUNTAIN SPRINGS CHURCH, Rapid City, South Dakota

*Wesleyan District:*
Northwest

*Lead Pastor:*
Rev. David Kinnan

*Web Site:*
www.fountainspringschurch.com

*Weekend Attendance (2014):*
2,506

*Locations:*
3 locations
- West Location. 2100 N. Plaza Drive, Rapid City, SD (4 weekend services)
- East Location. 912 Centre Drive, Rapid City, SD (2 weekend services)
- Prison church. Fountain Springs has church locations in the Rapid City Minimum Prison and the Pennington County, SD, Jail

*2014 Ministry Year Conversions and Baptisms:*
- Conversions: 492
- Baptisms: 283

*Survey Responses:*
Does your church use a formalized evangelism program?

> We do not use a formal program produced by someone outside of our church.

If no, do you use a hybrid program of your own?

> We don't have a program. Our DNA and culture at Fountain Springs is attractive to the non-believer. Our guest services, assimilation, sermon series, children's and youth services, music, and outreach are our way of reaching lost people. Our Mission is to show people who Jesus is. Since this is our mission and focus. We utilize four focuses to evangelize: Worship gatherings, Small Groups, Next Generation, and Serving.
>
> **In the past 8 years:**
> - Weekend worship attendance grew (from 140 people to 3,900+ today)
> - 5,679 people have been saved
> - 1,810 people have been baptized
>
> We have seen many people making decisions for Christ, and we have seen our church being a huge influence in the community.

Briefly describe how the typical person finds Jesus Christ as Savior at your church:

> Usually, a person finds Jesus through one of our weekend gatherings. We have 3 locations, one of them being in a local prison. Once a person responds to Jesus Christ and surrenders their life, they give us their information. Our staff and volunteers connect with this person and help them plug into community either through serving or

*joining a small group. We value these two opportunities because people are able to connect with other people to do life with, and it's our conviction that discipleship happens in relationship.*

**Note:**

Fountain Springs has this mission statement on their website: "At Fountain Springs Church we are one church with multiple locations focused on showing people who Jesus is. We are individuals who are unique in appearances, backgrounds, experiences, preferences and opinions; but together we're a community of believers worshipping the same God. Our weekend services are about 65 minutes each and are specifically designed to be fun with a creative and inviting atmosphere. As our guest, you can check out our services without intrusion and begin your spiritual journey at your own pace. We will be there to offer you opportunities and encouragement along the way." Fountain Springs' goal is to be one church with five locations by the end of 2016.

Fountain Springs has small groups (called FS Groups). To start groups, the church invites people to "find their four." People interested in leading a group are encouraged to "find four people, invite them together for 6 weeks, hang out and talk about God." The church offers an orientation to equip interested leaders and a team to walk beside them Fountain Springs offers four types of groups: Study Groups, Activity Groups, Recovery Groups and Classes.

# KINGS VALLEY WESLEYAN CHURCH, Quispamsis, New Brunswick, Canada

*Wesleyan District:*

Atlantic

*Lead Pastor:*

Rev. Brent Intersoll

*Web Site:*

www.kingsvalley.ca

*Weekend Attendance (2014):*

1,024

*Locations:*

2 locations
- Valley Campus, 332 Hampton Road, Quispamsis, NB (3 weekend services)
- East SJ Campus, 175 McAllister Drive, Saint John, NB (1 weekend service)

*2014 Ministry Year Conversions and Baptisms:*
- Conversions: 230
- Baptisms: 61

*Survey Responses:*

Does your church use a formalized evangelism program?

*No*

If no, do you use a hybrid program of your own?

*No, we have no standardized program.*

Briefly describe how the typical person finds Jesus Christ as Savior at your church:

*About 80% of our salvations happen in response times in our main services. The other 20% happen through personal evangelism, Celebrate Recovery and a few other outliers.*

**Note:**

Kings Valley's website has a strong evangelism statement under their "resources" tab titled "What does it mean to follow Jesus." It is a comprehensive guide to coming to know Christ, and can be accessed it at kingsvalley.ca/resources/follow-jesus/

## LIFE STREAM CHURCH, Allendale, Michigan

**Wesleyan District:**
West Michigan

**Lead Pastor:**
Rev. Jim Maness

**Web Site:**
www.lifestreamweb.org/

**Weekend Attendance (2014):**
907

**Locations:**
1 location
- 6561 Lake Michigan Drive, Allendale, MI

**2014 Ministry Year Conversions and Baptisms:**
- Conversions: 82
- Baptisms: 47

**Survey Responses:**

Does your church use a formalized evangelism program?

> We do not use a formal program, although we will rotate in a session of "Just Walk Across the Room" by Bill Hybels every now and again. We do evangelism training with people on a quarterly basis at what we call "Deep End." This is for those who consider themselves "all in" at Life Stream. This is a 15 minute time that we devote to do evangelism training with everyone here, and we have between 60 to 100 people who attend.

If no, do you use a hybrid program of your own?

*Training those who are highly committed to our church family on a quarterly basis has strongly developed friendship evangelism. We have also been able to highlight the variety of areas in which people have strengths and ask people to evangelize through their strengths. This works well, but we do believe we need to offer a more in-depth evangelism model for those who so desire.*

Briefly describe how the typical person finds Jesus Christ as Savior at your church:

*Sunday mornings often have a call to salvation in the following ways: 1) an appropriate place in the message, 2) in the call to communion once a month. We also have invitations to "baptism on the spot" 3 times a year on Sunday mornings, and two baptism experiences in Lake Michigan in the summer on Sunday evenings. People respond well to this type of call: "For those of you who have become a child of God and want to declare it to God and the World, this is your opportunity to do so." We have baptized an average of 50 people a year the past 3 years.*

*The use of welcome cards that are turned in during the offering have three different ways we can facilitate follow up with people who either 1) want to more about following Christ, 2) have made a decision to follow Christ, or 3) who would like to more about baptism. When people turn in a card, we set up a face-to-face moment with them. This face-to-face moment is scheduled after a Sunday morning worship experience. We refer to this as a "scheduled altar call." The person has just been in God's presence, and if we meet with them following the final morning service we are unrushed to converse with them about spiritual matters of faith and eternity. For some people we will set up a coffee conversation, but we love having scheduled altar calls with people whom God is working.*

**Note:**

Life Stream, a growing and highly relevant church, refers to themselves as a 164-year old church plant. The church was established in 1851 by 9 founding members meeting in a West Michigan farm house. They recently acquired a large school building on the main street of Allendale, Michigan, near the campus of a large state university, and have turned it into a beautiful state of the art worship and community center.

# NEW HOPE CHURCH, Durham, North Carolina

**Wesleyan District:**
North Carolina East

**Lead Pastor:**
Dr. Benji Kelley

**Web Site:**
www.newhopechurch.org/

**Weekend Attendance (2014):**
4,238

**Locations:**
7 locations in North and South Carolina, and 1 location in Kenya
- Central Campus. 7619 Fayetteville Rd, Durham, NC 27713
- Coffeehouse Campus. (located at the Central Campus building)
- Garner Campus. 2967 Benson Road, Garner, NC 27529
- Hillsborough Campus. 512 US-70, Hillsborough, NC 27278
- North Raleigh Campus. 6551 Meridien Drive, Suite 131, Raleigh, NC 27616
- Sanford Campus. 2901 Beechtree Drive, Sanford, NC 27330
- Columbia Campus. 930 Longtown Road, Columbia, SC, 29229
- Kenya Campus. YMCA building, Thika, Kenya.

**2014 Ministry Year Conversions and Baptisms:**
- Conversions: 1,679
- Baptisms: 276

**Survey Responses:**

Does your church use a formalized evangelism program?

> *Occasionally*

If yes, which ones do you use?

> *Just Walk Across the Room and Contagious Christianity*

How are these programs working for you?

> *Great! These were sermon series!*

Do you use a hybrid program of your own?

> *We are always thinking about how to encourage and challenge people to "invite and invest."*

Briefly describe your program.

> *We use invite cards, mailers, sermon series, etc.*

How is this program working for you?

> *Great when the preaching reinforces evangelism and outreach.*

Briefly describe how they typical person finds Jesus Christ as Savior at your church.

*See above for outreach. We also have Gospel centered sermons and clear invitation.*

**Note:**

New Hope Church is a fast-growing, fourteen-year-old church. They describe themselves as "an organic network of small groups meeting in people's homes throughout the week. They just happen to come together once a week on Sunday mornings to celebrate and worship God." New Hope's LifeGroups meet in semesters with short breaks in-between. They generally meet in a 3 on/1 off cycle, but this is open to the individual groups. There are five basic types of groups:

- Men's groups
- Women's groups
- Single's groups
- Couple's groups
- Everybody groups

Congregants can sign up for groups on-line during an open enrollment period. There is also a scheduled event called GroupLink where those interested in joining a group can meet group leaders and others who are interested in joining a group. Finally, there is a LifeGroup Expo held after Sunday morning services where those interested may explore current group offerings.

All LifeGroups follow the sermon-based study guides which are written by New Hope's staff.

New Hope Church has a program called "*Starting Point,*" which is for Seekers, Starters, and Returners. Seekers are those who are curious about God, Jesus and the Bible. Starters are those who have just begun a relationship with Christ. And

Returners are those who have some church experience, but have been a way for a while. This is an 8-week journey to lead the class participants into a growing relationship with Christ, by creating an open and accepting environment where they can explore faith and experience community. Starting Point is for those with questions about faith and those who want to learn more about the Bible and Christianity. There is a study guide for the class, and registration is $10 per person. To learn more about Starting Point, go to this link: www.newhopechurch.org/?s=starting+point.

## RED CEDAR CHURCH, Rice Lake, Wisconsin

**Wesleyan District:**
Wisconsin

**Lead Pastor:**
Rev. Heather Semple

**Web Site:**
www.redcedarchurch.com/

**Weekend Attendance (2014):**
950

**Locations:**
1 location
- 1701 W. Allen Street, Rice Lake, WI (3 weekend services)

**2014 Ministry Year Conversions and Baptisms:**
- Conversions: 307
- Baptisms: 206

**Survey Responses:**
Does your church use a formalized evangelism program?

*We began using the Alpha program in 2015 as part of our Next Steps system*

How are these programs working for you?

*We use the Alpha curriculum for our "Discover Faith" class. This class is a part of our next steps system which* also includes "Discover Red Cedar" and then moves people into Full Life Groups.

Do you use a hybrid program of your own?

*Everything we do is oriented to reaching people for Jesus Christ — including programs such as our fall kickoff (Red Cedar Fest), Christmas and Eastser Services and Outreach Programs (specifically focusing on justice-involved populations including foster families and people returning from jail/prison and community-wide events like Love Week and our Back to School bash.*

Briefly describe how they typical person finds Jesus Christ as Savior at your church.

*We minister to people from every social and economic class. Our slogan of "Everyone's Welcome — Nobody's Perfect — Anything's Possible" has a unique appeal to people who have felt like they have not traditionally fit (or been welcomed) in church. We see many first-time adult salvations following our major programmatic pushes (Red Cedar Fest in the fall, Christmas, Easter, etc.). We also regularly talk to our children and youth about having a personal relationship with Jesus Christ. In the fiscal year 2015-2016 we experienced 759 salvations and 516 baptisms.*

**Note:**

Located in the north woods of Wisconsin, Red Cedar Church was chosen for this survey for their 2014 ministry year salvations and baptisms (307 conversions and 206 baptisms).

However, their 2015 results were even more dynamic with 709 salvations and 516 baptisms. Red Cedar Church is definitely a church on the move. In May of 2015 they moved into a new building with 1,751 people attending their Grand Opening service. Current attendance, in 2016, is 1,400 people, up from an average of 950 in 2014. Attendance at Easter was 2,989 people. And this is in a town of only 9,000 people. Their mission statement, Everybody's Welcome — Nobody's Perfect — Anything's Possible definitely resonates with the community. Everything Red Cedar accomplishes is done with the thought of evangelizing their community and the world.

Red Cedar has a full spectrum of small groups and classes. Their Full Life Groups meet and discuss the weekend's message, explore issues like parenting and marriage, and pray for and encourage each other.

They also have a program called Specialty Groups. These groups meet for a short period of time and explore one topic. Current Specialty Groups are:

- Financial Peace University
- Discover FAITH
- Membership Class
- The Daniel Plan
- Marriage Focus Group
- How to Study Your Bible
- The Marriage Course

In addition to these two categories, there is another called Care Groups. These groups include:

- Divorce Care
- Grief Share

- AA
- Sexaholics Anonymous
- Pure (men's group for sexual purity)

Red Cedar has several annual outreach events. One is their Back to School Bash where community children are invited in to receive free backpacks, free clothes and free haircuts. Food is served. The event is held on a Saturday in August from 10:00 AM to 12:30 PM.

Under the "Outreach" section of Red Cedar's website is this statement: "Red Cedar Church exists to lead people to a full life in Jesus. As a church we believe in going outside our walls to partner with our community to demonstrate God's love. We are currently working alongside law enforcement to learn how to better serve in our jail systems. We are also partnering with the Foster Care system in Barron."

**Global Outreach:**
Red Cedar is working with the Trash Mountain Project. This organization is making an impact for the kingdom of God by working with communities who live, work and die in trash dump communities worldwide. They provide discipleship, education, healthcare, nutrition, work and housing to these families and children.

# SKYLINE WESLEYAN CHURCH, La Mesa, California

**Wesleyan District:**
Pacific Southwest

**Lead Pastor:**
Dr. Jim Garlow

**Web Site:**
www.skylinechurch.org/

**Weekend Attendance (2014):**
2,376

**Locations:**
1 location.
- 11330 Campo Road, La Mesa, California.
  (6 weekend services)
  Weekend services
  - Saturdays. 10:00 AM Tree of Life Messianic Congregation Service
  - Sunday mornings. 8:30 AM and 10:30 AM
  - Sunday mornings. 8:30 AM Traditional Worship in the Chapel
  - Sunday evenings. 6:00 PM Young Adults Service
  - Sunday afternoons. 1:00 PM Hispanic Bilingual Service

**2014 Ministry Year Conversions and Baptisms:**
- Conversions: 210
- Baptisms: 81

**Survey Responses:**

Does your church use a formalized evangelism program?

> *In the past we have used Evangelism Explosion and the Roman Road. We just had Tom Mercer speak on Sunday morning and then did an OIKOS seminar on Sunday night.*

If yes, which ones do you use?

> **OIKOS (new for us)** *[see an explanation of OIKOS in the "notes" section on the next page]*

How are these programs working for you?

> *We are seeing some results with people coming to faith in Jesus. We have a team that goes to the beach once a month to barbeque hot dogs and then share Christ using Evangelism Explosion. We utilize the booklet "Would You Like to Know Christ Personally." We are in a 3-week follow-up series to the OIKOS message Tom Mercer gave 2 weeks ago. We are scheduled to have Kevin Harney at Skyline Church on November 13-14, 2016, regarding "Organic Outreach" He will preach on Sunday morning and then do training sessions with our key leaders on Sunday and Monday nights.*

Briefly describe how the typical person finds Jesus Christ as Savior at your church.

> *Our pastor usually gives an invitation at the end of the service for people to respond to the message and to accept Jesus Christ into their lives. They are encouraged*

> to come and visit our Evangelism Team at our Guest Service area after the service where we give them follow-up materials, get their information for further follow-up and pray with them. Invitations to accept Christ are given on a regular basis in all areas of our ministries from children to adults.
>
> We have had training classes on witnessing and evangelism giving them the tools to use to share Christ with their neighbors, co-workers and friends.
>
> Our desire is for our congregation to become more intentional in sharing their love for God and with those they come in contact with. Utilizing the OIKOS concept and Organic Outreach materials will help us accomplish that goal. We need to get away from people seeing the church building as a "soul saving station."

**Note:**

Skyline Church uses the OIKOS concept of evangelism. OIKOS is a program developed by Tom Mercer. On the OIKOS website we find the statement: "Jesus sets apart, prepares and commissions His Church to be ambassadors for the message of the Cross, to continue His ministry of reconciliation to the lost; and He both modeled and taught a strategic formula that would facilitate that great endeavor. From the beginning of His redemptive plan, God has consistently focused on a specific group, the *oikos* (as the Greeks called it) as His primary target for evangelism. That is, He primarily perpetuates His Kingdom through those close social connections that we all have, those eight to fifteen people He strategically placed around each one of us in our own relational worlds." The OIKOS Challenge is as follows:

- Find a small group of believers who also want to help the people around them discover the difference that Jesus has made in your lives.
- Make a group commitment to get together once a week for three weeks.
- Each week, use the resources Tom [Mercer] has developed to help you refocus your life around the people God has brought to your doorstep. Read the book, answer the questions, watch the three DVD presentations, fill out the cards and discuss what it means to be a world-changer.

The OIKOS website can be found here: www.8to15.com/

Skyline Wesleyan Church was founded in 1954 by Dr. Orval Butcher. He remained their pastor for 27 years. Dr. Butcher was followed by John Maxwell, the author of many books on business, leadership and Christian living, and is currently the President of INJOY, which provides leadership tools to pastors and lay leaders. The current pastor, Dr. Jim Garlow, has been at Skyline since 1995.

Skyline has a robust small group program, listing 108 small groups on their website for adults, teens and children. They have groups for almost every interest including a quilting group, a Wild Wings group (for men), recovery groups, general Bible studies, couples and singles groups, fitness groups, divorce care, and other groups for all ages. For a complete list of Skyline's groups, link to: www.skylinechurch.org/smallgroups/#.

In addition to small groups, Skyline offers Connect Classes. The current classes listed are:

- Entrepreneuring for Christ (This discussion forum for business owners, leaders and professional people focuses on how to integrate our work plans with God's plan.)
- Young at Heart (55+)
- New Venture (this class studies from one to several books of the Bible each year)
- Family Life Class
- Applying the Bible to Culture (discusses current cultural topics)
- Live, Love, Laugh, Learn (general Bible study)
- Forbidden Table Talk (controversial questions discussed)
- 2 Become 1 (a marriage enrichment class)
- To Be Made New (a class for women only focused on finding identity in Christ)
- Skyline Adult Singles 35+
- 101 Encounter (this new discussion-based course helps both new and seasoned believers explore the essentials of the faith, form deep relationships, and invest in life at Skyline)

Here is a link to Skyline's classes: www.skylinechurch.org/connectclasses/

CHAPTER 12

# Concluding notes from Wes: Rethinking and Rebuilding a Culture of Evangelism

It has become a tradition at Daybreak to, each summer, do a message series called Jesus at the Movies. Our teaching team takes a popular movie and uses it as a backdrop to teach spiritual truth, much the same as Jesus used parables.

One summer, I used a 2013 movie called *Gravity*, which is about a veteran astronaut, Matt Kowalski, played by George Clooney, and a medical engineer, Dr. Ryan Stone, played by Sandra Bullock. They work together in an effort to survive after a catastrophic collision with space debris destroys their shuttle, leaving them adrift in orbit.

The message was built around the following words delivered by Dr. Stone when she believed she was about to die.

> "Oh, I'm going to die. I know we're all gonna die. Everybody knows that. But I'm going to die today! It's funny that… you know, to know. But the thing is, that I'm still scared. Really scared. No one will mourn for me, no one will pray for my soul. Will you mourn for me? Will you say a prayer for me? Or is it too late… ah, I'd say one for myself but I've never really prayed in

my life. Nobody ever taught me how... Nobody ever taught me how . . ." *(Cuaron, 2013)*

In the Introduction, I mentioned that my father had attended a tent revival meeting and was confronted with the claims of Christ. Like Dr. Stone, no one had ever taught my dad how to pray. Fortunately, the next evening the young soldier from Fort Knox, Bruce Meads, helped my dad to pray.

That scene from *Gravity* still haunts me. She believes she is going to die, and no one had ever taught her how to pray. No one had ever showed any interest in her soul. But someone should have. How many millions of people are in a comparable situation? Facing death and hopeless, they are adrift. No one has ever shared the Gospel with them. No one has ever taught them how to pray.

Where do we start in cultivating a culture of evangelism? How do we teach someone to pray - to invite Jesus Christ into their lives? Let me be honest: This doesn't come easy. It is definitely a supernatural thing. But you must also have a plan, and there must be effort on your part.

So, now it is your turn. Here are some thoughts:

### #1. It starts with you.

C.H. Spurgeon said: "The Holy Spirit will move them by moving you. If you can rest without their being saved, they will rest too. But if you are filled with an agony for them; if you cannot bear that they should be lost, you will soon find that they are uneasy too. I hope you will get into such a state that you will dream about your child or your hearer perishing for lack of Christ, and start up at once and begin to cry, 'O God, give me converts or I die!' Then you will have converts." *(Spurgeon, 2017, pp. 143-144)*

### #2. No more excuses.

You might say, "But I'm not a Billy Graham or a Clyde Dupin! I'm just a minister (or just a teacher, or just a carpenter, or just an electrician, or just, just just)." That may be true, but Paul told Timothy, a young, inexperienced man, to "do the work of an evangelist." *(2 Timothy 4:5, NIV)*

Imagine you are hearing the Gospel for the first time. How would you want it explained to you? Keep it simple and keep it short; but share it. It is said that Billy Graham would, in his preaching, articulate the Gospel in such a way that even a 12-year old could understand it.

### #3. If you are a pastor, start giving public invitations.

I would often hear my dad, at the time of his invitations, refer to Jesus' method of calling people. He would say, "Every person that Jesus called, He called them publicly. So, I am calling you to come to Christ the same way." Public invitations are important. During a session at the Billy Graham School of Evangelism in 1972, in Cleveland, Ohio, we were instructed to observe how soon into his message Billy would begin his invitation. He would start the invitation soon after he began the message. Whether you are teaching or preaching, do so with urgency and expectation. I have heard my dad many times quote the Apostle Peter when he said, "Each of you must repent of your sins and turn to God!" *(Acts 2:37-39 NLT)* Billy Graham always preached for decisions.

### #4. Explain to the congregation how the invitation will work.

I have observed ministers begin their invitation well, and then drop the ball. Be sure to make the invitation clear, and make the audience aware of what you are asking them to do. It might be simply filling out a card, or standing up, or raising their hand, or talking with a prayer counselor at the close of the service, or inviting them to come forward. Make the "decision time method" clear.

### #5. Have "next steps" in place.

I've trained thousands of people in how to lead others to Christ; and have also taught them how to follow up after a decision was reached. My dad wrote a little book for follow-up. It contained five lessons on beginning in their new faith, and how to make their journey with Christ work. It was called "Grow in Christ," and was very simply written. If you don't have a follow-up plan, develop one and start using it.

### #6. Develop a continuing culture of evangelism.

We live on a small lake, and I enjoy using my Sea-Doo™. It's nothing fancy, but it goes fast. One year I put it away for the winter, but failed to keep the battery charged. When summer arrived, I pulled it out of storage and, when I put it in the water, it was dead. Finally, after unsuccessfully trying to start it, I headed to the local repair shop. They looked it over and said there were no mechanical problems, but that the spark plug had gone bad over the winter and, as a result, the battery had died. We added a new spark plug and a new battery, and it fired right up. Like my little watercraft, people can grow tired and weary and often return to mediocrity, and their evangelism spark will die if it is not tended to. They must be constantly reminded that evangelism is a key core value of the church.

Each September, I do a series called "Table Talk." On the stage is a dining room table with four chairs around it. Each chair symbolizes a different stage in the spiritual life of people within the church. As we talk about each chair, I explain that one of the most important chairs is the first one; the chair which represents the person who has no faith in Christ. Does this person get invited to the table? Do they feel welcome? Do we freely share the food (the Gospel) with them? Or are there some of them who do not feel welcome at the table because of the way they dress, the way they talk, or the tattoos they sport? I explain how we must first invest in their lives, and then invite them. Once they come to church, we must then make them feel welcome, giving them both space and permission to ask questions. I then share with the congregation how to present the gospel in a simple manner and lead them in a very simple "sinner's prayer."

Evangelism is what every follower of Jesus Christ should be engaged in on a regular basis. This means sharing their faith, leading others to Christ, discipling them, and helping them to become grounded in the local church. And then going out and doing it all over again.

Whenever the topic of evangelism is brought up, people cringe. I find many times both the believer and the unbeliever are uptight about it. But the fact remains that Jesus said, "Go into all the world and preach the Good News to everyone." *(Mark 16:15, NLT)* This is a command, not a suggestion. And it's from Jesus himself. It is the Great Commission.

The church in America has had many starts and stops when it comes to evangelism. We have, at times, come so close to success — close enough to be called "an almost chosen people." But "almost" isn't good enough. It's time to reignite the spark and finish the job. So, let the adventure begin!

# Acknowledgements from Wes

I want to acknowledge and thank the One who spoke to my heart as a 10-year old boy and saved me.

I want to thank my best friend, Claudia — my high school sweetheart and cheerleader who I had the privilege of leading to Christ — the one who always stands by me and supports me. I could not do ministry without you.

Thank you to my wonderful sons and their wives: Chad and Sara, Clint and Michaell. I love you with all my heart and I am so proud of the way you are raising our grandchildren to love and follow Jesus.

Thank you to my parents. Clyde and Grace Dupin. I am who I am because of the life you lived before me. You taught me how to be passionate about evangelism.

Thanks to Wayne Schmidt who believed in me and invited Claudia and me to West Michigan to start this new church called Daybreak.

Thank you, Bill Hybels, for teaching us how to invest our lives in people far from God.

Thank you, Ed and Lisa Young, for showing us how to do church creatively and with excellence.

Thanks to John and Craig Dunn for taking a financial risk on our vision for a great church. We could not have done it without you.

Thank you, JoAnne Lyon, for believing in me so much you appointed me to represent the Wesleyan Denomination on the newly-formed Evangelism Leaders Fellowship led by Ed Stetzer, the Billy Graham Distinguished Chair of Evangelism, Wheaton College.

Thank you, Jim Dunn for spending a day strategizing how we could lead the Wesleyan Church and other denominations to go to a whole new level of evangelism.

Thank you, Kevin and Sherry Harney, for your love, support and friendship. You are two of the greatest evangelists and prayer warriors I know.

Thank you, Anita Eastlack, for taking evangelism and discipleship seriously. You are invaluable to the Wesleyan Church, and to us.

Thank you, Mary Merrill, Mark Courtney, Jeff Gifford, Frank Gutbrod and Katie Long who invested many hours of challenging work to make this book happen.

Special thanks to Ramona Way for her countless hours reviewing our manuscript. Her eye for detail is amazing and her suggestions are spot on. If you really don't want to know what she thinks of your writing, don't ask her to review it!

With gratitude to the staffs of 12Stone Church, Celebrate Community Church, Fountain Springs Church, Kings Valley

## Acknowledgements from Wes

Wesleyan, Lifestream Church, New Hope Church, Red Cedar Church, and Skyline Wesleyan Church for taking the time to answer our pesky survey questions. But even more, thank you for your commitment to sharing the Gospel with lost people in your communities and our world. You are awesome!

Thanks to Steve Dunmire of Houghton College, Stephen Elliott of Kingswood University, Bonita Wuertley, Paul Gaverick, Dave Ward and Ken Schenck of Indiana Wesleyan University, Mari Gonlag and Dave Tolen of Southern Wesleyan University, and Jim Dunn and the team at Oklahoma Wesleyan University in helping obtain syllabi for evangelism courses; and to Kris Dekker and Mark Wilson for their assistance in obtaining the information from Flame.

Thanks to Ron McClung from the Wesleyan Denomination Headquarters for sharing attendance and conversions figures for the Wesleyan Church. This provided the basis for our statistical analysis.

Thank you to Terry and Shelly Woychowski for your close friendship and continued encouragement. Your reward is great in Heaven.

Thanks to Bob and Lynne LeHocky for your deep friendship from the beginning of Daybreak. Bob, you often remind me that I led you to Jesus.

Special thanks to Norm and Margaret Lam for helping me start Daybreak and developing evangelism as one of our core values right from the beginning.

Thank you, Denny and Jean Jonker Sr., for your prayer and support. You are two of the greatest givers I have ever known.

Thank you, Tim Way, for putting so many of my ideas in writing, helping to challenge others with a vision for evangelism.

Thank you, Walt Grzybowski, Harv Westmaas and Craig Geers, for backpacking hundreds of miles through rugged mountains and valleys; and just for being best friends who love to share their stories of how Christ has transformed their lives.

Thank you, Steve Frody, for leading the evangelism charge at Daybreak. You are awesome!

Thank you, Kyle Clausen and John LaBarge, for your great leadership, and making it possible to have one of the great church facilities that attracts the unchurched and people far from God.

Thank you, Mike Smith, for all your counsel and wisdom on building a church for those far from God. Mike was my very first band member and worship leader at Daybreak.

Finally, thank you Daybreak Church. Never have I seen a group of people hungrier for God, and more willing to invest and invite their friends and family members who are lost. You are willing to do whatever it takes to reach people for Christ, and are an example to believers all over the world. I thank God for choosing me to be your pastor.

And eternal gratitude to our Savior, Jesus Christ, for allowing us the privilege of partnering with Him in scattering seeds. We scatter, but He brings the harvest.

# Bibliography

*Aimee Semple McPherson.* (n.d.). Retrieved May 18, 2015, from The Biography.com website: www.biography.com/people/aim%C3%A9e-semple-mcpherson-9394517

Anderson, G. H. (1998). *Thomas Coke.* Retrieved April 29, 2015, from Boston University School of Theology: www.bu.edu/missiology/missionary-biography/c-d/coke-thomas-1747-1814/

*Anne Johnson.* (1994). Retrieved October 27, 2015, from Encyclopedia.com: www.encyclopedia.com/doc/1G2-2870700014.html

Armstrong, C. (2008, August 8). *Christian History.* Retrieved August 18, 2015, from Christianity Today: www.christianitytoday.com/ch/news/2003/jun20.html

*BGCE at Wheaton College.* (n.d.). Retrieved August 26, 2015, from Wheaton College: www.wheaton.edu/BGCE

*Bill Glass.* (n.d.). Retrieved May 19, 2015, from Billglass.org website: www.billglass.org/about_BillGlass.cfm

*Billy Graham.* (n.d.). Retrieved May 18, 2015, from The Biography.com website: www.biography.com/people/billy-graham-9317669

*Billy Sunday.* (n.d.). Retrieved May 18, 2015, from Wheaton College Institute for the Study of American Evangelicals: www.wheaton.edu/isae/hall-of-biography/billy-sunday

Black, M. (2015, April 23). Flame Evangelism Class Syllabus. (K. Dekker, Interviewer)

*Bob Jones Sr.* (n.d.). Retrieved May 19, 2015, from Institute for the Study of American Evangelicals, Wheaton College: www.wheaton.edu/isae/hall-of-biography/bob-jones-sr

Butler, J. (1990). *Awash in a Sea of Faith.* Cambridge, Massachusetts: Harvard University Press.

Caldwell, W. E. (1992). *Reformers and Revivalists: The History of the Wesleyan Church.* Indianapolis, Indiana: Wesley Press.

Chismer, J. (2010, November 10). *Remembering the Legacy of Howard O. Jones.* Retrieved October 27, 2015, from Billy Graham Evangelistic Association: www.billygraham.org/story/remembering-the-legacy-of-howard-o-jones/

*Christian Biography Resources: R. A. Torrey.* (2015). Retrieved October 27, 2015, from Wholesome Words: www.wholesomewords.org/biography/bioratorrey.html

*Clyde Dupin.* (n.d.). Retrieved May 19, 2015, from Clyde Dupin Ministries website: www.clydedupin.org/dupin.html

Counsel of the Pilgrim Holiness Church. (1922). *Manual of the Pilgrim Holiness Church.* Easton, Maryland: The Easton Publishing Company.

Covell, R. R. (2008). *Missionary Biography: J. Hudson Taylor.* Retrieved April 30, 2015, from Boston University School of Theology.

Cuaron, A. (Director). (2013). *Gravity* [Motion Picture].

*D. L. Moody's Story.* (n.d.). Retrieved May 17, 2015, from Moody Bible Institute: www.moody.edu/dl-moody/

*Department of Evangelism and Missions.* (2015). Retrieved August 26, 2015, from Southern Baptist Theological

Seminary: http://www.sbts.edu/bgs/evangelism-and-missions/

Doucet, C. W. (2002, June). *Ryerson Biography*. Retrieved April 30, 2015, from Ryerson Library Archives: www.library.ryerson.ca/asc/archives/ryerson-history/ryerson-bio/

Doyle, G. W. (2013). *Christianity In America: Triumph and Tragedy*. Wipf and Stock Publishers.

Drury, R. B. (2012). *Story of the Wesleyan Church*. Indianapolis, Indiana: Wesleyan Publishing House.

Dunmire, S. (2015, December 18). Syllabus for Houghton College Evangelism Class. Houghton, New York.

Elliott, S. (2015, October 8). Kingswood University Evangelism Syllabi.

*Evangelist Oral Roberts dead at 91*. (2009, December 16). Retrieved October 27, 2015, from CNN: www.cnn.com/2009/US/12/15/oral.roberts/

Findings Committee, Second Session. (1970). *Findings Committee*, (p. 1). Indianapolis, Indiana. Retrieved May 26, 2015

*Finney*. (n.d.). Retrieved April 20, 2015, from University of Virginia: http://xroads.virginia.edu/~Hyper/DETOC/religion/finney.html

*Franklin Graham*. (n.d.). Retrieved May 18, 2015, from Samaritan's Purse International Relief website: www.samaritanspurse.org/our-ministry/franklin-graham-biography/

Graves, D. (2007, June). *Philip Embury, America's 1st Methodist Pastor*. Retrieved April 20, 2015, from Christianity.com: www.christianity.com/church/church-history/timeline/1701-1800/philip-embury-americas-1st-methodist-pastor-11630270.html

Hadaway, Kirk, P. M. (2005). *How Many Americans Attend Worship Each Week? An Alternative Approach to Measurement.* Retrieved August 19, 2015, from Journal for the Scientific Study of Religion: www.wiley.com/wiley/cda

Heck, Barbara. (2010, February 10). Retrieved May 11, 2015, from Appletons' Cyclopedia of American Biography/ Heck, Barbara: http://en.wikisource.org/wiki/Appletons%27_Cyclop%C3%A6dia_of_American_Biography/Heck,_Barbara

Hill, B. (1980). *Clyde Dupin, Born to be the Evangelist.* Mt. Juliet, Tennesse: Cross Reference Books.

*Honoring Excellence in Evangelism.* (2014). Retrieved August 24, 2015, from Foundation for Evangelism: www.foundationforevangelism.org/grants/distinguisned-evangelist-award

*Hyman Jedidiah Appleman.* (2003, March 13). Retrieved October 27, 2015, from Believer's Web: http://www.believersweb.org/view.cfm?id=98&rc=1&list=multi

*James and Betty Robison.* (2015). Retrieved October 27, 2015, from Life Today: http://lifetoday.org/about-life/james-and-betty-robison/

Kinnell, M. (n.d.). *Ford Philpot.* Retrieved October 27, 2015, from Asbury University: www.asbury.edu/offices/library/archives/biographies/ford-philpot

Lain, D. E. (2009). *Evangelism Strategies for Reaching Pre-Christians in Upstate New York.* Kansas City, Missouri: Asbury Theological Seminary. Retrieved May 26, 2015

*Leighton Ford Ministries.* (2015). Retrieved October 27, 2015, from Leigthton Ford Ministries: http://leightonfordministries.org/about-2/

*Liberty University Master of Arts in Christian Ministry.* (2015). Retrieved August 26, 2015, from Liberty University Online: www.liberty.edu/online/masters/christian-ministry/

*Luis Palau.* (n.d.). Retrieved May 18, 2015, from About.com website: http://christianity.about.com/od/christiancelebrities/p/luispalau.htm

MacBeth, Wayne, R. M. (Ed.). (2012). *Discipline of the Wesleyan Church*. Indianapolis: Wesleyan Publishing House.

Marty, M. (1984). *Pilgrims in Their Own Land*. London, England: Penguin Books, Ltd.

Maxey, R. D. (1998). *Captain Thomas Webb*. Retrieved May 11, 2015, from Wesleyan Heritage Library: Biographies: www.google.com/url?sa=t&rct=j&q=&esrc=s&source=web&cd=10&ved=0CD8QFjAJ&url=http%3A%2F%2Fmedia.sabda.org%2Falkitab-6%2Fwh2-hdm%2Fhdm0211.pdf&ei=fEpRVePuC4OXsAWtn4GACQ&usg=AFQjCNFCYpgv3v9Gl3w00MJmibvn66ZJBQ

McClung, R. (n.d.). The Wesleyan Church: Spreadsheet of Conversions/Churches/Attendance. (R. McClung, Compiler) Retrieved April 16, 2015

McCullough, D. (2001). *John Adams*. New York: Simon & Schuster, Inc.

McLeister, I. (1976). *Conscience and Commitment: The History of the Wesleyan Methodist Church in America* (4th Edition ed.). (L. J. Haines, Ed.) Marion, Indiana: The Wesley Press.

Minutes of the Findings Committee, February 5-7. (1970). *Minutes of the Findings Committee, Conference on Evangelism*. Marion, Indiana. Retrieved May 26, 2015

Mitchell, V. A. (1984). Pastoral Letter. *Journal of the Fifth General Conference of the Wesleyan Church*, (pp. 224-225). Columbus, Ohio.

Mordecai Ham. (n.d.). Retrieved April 15, 2015, from Ranker.com website: www.ranker.com/list/list-of-famous-evangelists/reference

Mull, M. (1996). Report of the General Director of Evangelism and Church Growth. *Journal of the Eighth Conference of the Wesleyan Church.* Indianapolis, Indiana: Wesley Press.

Obituaries. (1987, November 3). Retrieved October 27, 2015, from New York Times: www.nytimes.com/1987/11/03/obituaries/grady-b-wilson.html

Pence, J. G. (2012). Report of the Interim Director of the Department of Evangelism and Church Growth. *Conference Journal of the Twelfth General Conference of the Wesleyan Church.* Lexington, Kentucky: Wesleyan Publishing House.

Philbrick, N. (2006). *Mayflower.* New York: Penguin Group.

(1970). *Planning Guide: 100 Days.* Indianapolis, Indiana: The Wesleyan Church. Retrieved May 26, 2015

Plemmons, D. (n.d.). *Pilgrim Holiness Church - About Us.* Retrieved May 10, 2015, from Pilgrim Holiness Church - Midwest: www.midwestphc.org/index.html

Ray Comfort. (n.d.). Retrieved May 18, 2015, from Livingwaters.com website: www.livingwaters.com/biography/ray-comfort

Sawyer, J. C. (1984). Evangelism and Church Growth Report. *Journal of the Fifth General Conference of the Wesleyan Church*, (p. 311). Columbus, Ohio.

Schenck, K. (2012, October 15). *The Decade of Evangelism (1970's): Black and Drury.* Retrieved May 26, 2015, from Common Denominator: http://kenschenck.blogspot.com/2012/10/the-decade-of-evangelism-1970s-black.html

Schiff, S. (2015). *The Witches: Salem, 1692.* New York: Little, Brown and Company.

*School of Biblical Evangelism.* (n.d.). Retrieved August 26, 2015, from School of Biblical Evangelism: www.biblicalevangelism.com/page.php?id=344

*School of Evangelism Online.* (n.d.). Retrieved August 26, 2015, from Billy Graham Online Training: www.billygrahamonlinetraining.org/soe/courses/

Scott, C. O. (1970). Seminar - Pastor/Evangelist: A Team. *Conference on Evangelism*, (pp. 1 - 2). Cincinnati, Ohio. Retrieved May 26, 2015

Smith, G. (n.d.). *Gypsy Smith (1860-1947): His Life and Work.* Retrieved November 2, 2015, from Biblebelievers.com: www.biblebelievers.com/gypsy_smith/

*Spurgeon Archive.* (n.d.). Retrieved April 30, 2015, from The Spurgeon Archive: www.spurgeon.org/aboutsp.htm.

Spurgeon, C. (2017). *Spurgeon Sermons Preached and Revised.* London: Forgotten Books.

Stevenson, P. (2008). Report of the General Director of Evangelism and Church Growth. *Journal of the Eleventh General Conference of the Wesleyan Church.* Orlando, Florida: Wesleyan Publishing House.

Thomas, P. (1976). *Days of our Pilgrimage: The History of the Pilgrim Holiness Church.* Marion, Indiana: The Wesley Press.

Tipple, E. (2008, August 8). *Denominational Founders: Asbury.* Retrieved April 30, 2015, from Christianity Today: www.christianitytoday.com/ch/131christians/denominationalfounders/asbury.html

*Torrey Johnson.* (2015, January 19). Retrieved October 27, 2015, from Wikipedia: https://en.wikipedia.org/wiki/Torrey_Johnson

Uniting General Conference of the Wesleyan Church. (1968). *The Discipline of the Wesleyan Church.* Marion, Indiana: The Wesleyan Publishing House.

Weir, W. (2013, January 15). *Irish Methodist Genealogy.* Retrieved April 30, 2015, from Wordpress.com: https://irishmethodistgenealogy.wordpress.com/2013/01/15/gideon-ouseley-a-maverick-irish-methodist-preacher/

Wesleyan Methodist Connection. (1843). *Discipline of the Wesleyan Methodist Connection.* Boston: O. Scott, John S. Hall, Printer.

Wilson, E. L. (2008). Pastoral Letter. *Eleventh General Counsel of the Wesleyan Church.* Orlando, Florida: Wesleyan Publishing House.

Wilson, E. L. (2015, January 12). *Facebook.* Retrieved May 3, 2015, from Pilgrim Holiness History: www.facebook.com/permalink.php?story_fbid=379529218891208&id=365802563597207&substory_index=0

Withrow, W. H. (1898). *Makers of Methodism.* Toronto, Canada: William Briggs.

Wuertley, B. (2015, August 3). Syllabi for Evangelism Classes at Indiana Wesleyan University. Marion, Indiana.